WHAT AM I GOING TO DO WITH ALL THESE FISH?

A Kitchen Guide for Alaskan Sports Fisherman for Cooking Salmon and Halibut

by Tom Rinderer

Salmon Bayou Press

ISBN -13: 978-0692486139 (Salmon Bayou Press)

Additional copies available through salmonbayou.com

Dedication

This book is dedicated to my fishing partners, Bruce, Gary, Manly, Neil, Steve the Elder and Steve the Younger who helped catch all the fish; my chief tasters, Darwin and Janina, who ate their way through all the dishes of fish from my kitchen that both did and did not make the final list of recipes; and to my enthusiastic canine helpers, Kaffir and Utah, who always make sure that no scraps of fish go to waste.

A special thank you to Nancy Haver (nancyhaver.com) for her wonderful illustrations of Hal and Sam, to Steve "The Elder" Sheppard for permission to use the cover photo and to Janina Fuller and Frank Garza for providing editorial suggestions.

Forward

When I visited my friend Steve the Elder in Pullman, Washington in 2007 he gave me what seemed at the time to be an enormous amount of salmon and halibut (30 pounds) from his recent fishing trip to Alaska. Since my main hobby (aside from fishing) is cooking, I had great fun finding ways to prepare the fish. I thought that one of my halibut preparations was especially sensational.

I was delighted when Steve invited me to join his group on their next Alaskan fishing adventure. I was a bit stunned at the end of the trip when the fish cleaning house presented me with well over 100 pounds of frozen salmon and halibut fillets. How would I ever be able to use it all?

When I got the fish home, one of the first things I attempted to cook was the halibut dish I had made the year before. I was very frustrated when I could not recreate it as I remembered. So, I started to write down my recipes. This soon led to the idea of creating a cookbook for me and my Alaskan fishing partners. In the past eight years I have been creating, testing and revising this collection of recipes. As the book developed, it seemed that other Alaskan fisherman, their families and friends who share their catch might also find the recipes useful.

While anyone interested in cooking salmon and halibut will find new ideas and recipes in this cookbook, it is not intended to be an encyclopedia of salmon and halibut cooking. It is written primarily for the Alaskan fishing tourist. These fishermen enjoy one to several days of fishing, catching mainly salmon and halibut. Cleaning of their fish is usually done by commercial fish cleaning services that generally provide the fishermen with vacuum packed frozen fillets. The recipes that follow are designed to provide inspiration to turn an abundance of frozen fillets into varied and enjoyable meals that will enhance the Alaskan fishing experience.

The fillets from a salmon are about one-third of the weight of the whole fresh salmon. Most Alaskan fishing tourists take home only fillets because fillets are the most economical product to ship home by air as excess baggage. Fish parts that contain bones (whole fish, steaks, collars) are also wonderful for the kitchen. Many people find that the flesh near a bone is more flavorful. Some fish processing houses will also prepare bone-in products for transport if asked, although they may require additional fees.

Fillets from a halibut total a bit more than half of the weight of the whole fish. Without special arrangements, fish processing houses will also extract halibut cheeks for their clients. Halibut cheeks are considered by many chefs to be the finest product of the sea.

Because my home is in southern Louisiana, many of my recipes are inspired by Louisiana Cajun and Creole cooking. Since I also enjoy Thai and Italian food, some of the recipes feature Thai flavors or Italian preparations. I especially enjoy home-smoked salmon, and have therefore devoted an entire chapter to smoking techniques and another chapter to recipes that use smoked salmon.

Some of the recipes in this book are "upscale" and suitable for fancy dinner parties. But, for the most part, I do my cooking after work. So the majority of these recipes are easy and quick to prepare, although they also are worthy of being served to company.

The format of this book is designed to be helpful to the cook. Larger font makes reading from a distance easier. The ingredients are listed in the order that they are used and presented in bold italics so that the cook can look away and easily come back to the same place. The procedures are presented as distinct bullets.

I have very much enjoyed creating this book. I hope my readers have equal enjoyment in using it. I wish you successful fishing and, most especially, happy cooking!

Tom Rinderer, Summer 2015, Saint Gabriel, Louisiana

Table of Contents

Please obey fishing laws
so your grandchildren can fish.

Preparing the Catch for Shipping, Storage and Cooking

A quality fish product in the kitchen starts when a fish is first harvested. The moment a fish dies, it begins to lose its value for cooking. Of course, the bears and sea lions have the right idea; eat the fish at the moment of capture. However, humans are mostly content to take the fish home to the kitchen which may be many thousands of miles away. Generally, the better the fish is handled as a food the better food it will be.

On the Boat

It is common to see commercial fishermen on the water gutting their catch before placing the fish on ice for transport to the dock. Gutting a fish also drains blood from the meat of the fish, which improves the flavor when the fish is cooked. If a recreational fisherman is on a day trip and the fish will be cleaned shortly after landing, gutting and icing may not be necessary. However, bleeding, which can be done by cutting through the gills on preferably both sides, is essential. This greatly increases the flavor of the fish since fish blood in the meat reduces flavor quality. Once bled, the fish should be placed on ice if possible. Although weather conditions in Alaska are often cold and rainy, an open fish box on the boat with no ice is, at best, only as good as a refrigerator. Ice is far better at slowing the degradation of quality.

On the River

Ideally, a bled and gutted fish should be placed on ice shortly after it is caught. If the time until icing is prolonged (because, for example, your vehicle is a long walk from the river), gutting and bleeding are more important, and should be done in the water (as opposed to on the bank) so as not to attract bears. On the other hand, if other fishermen are present, it would be discourteous to contaminate the stream with fish offal (although the offal is organic and nature will soon make it disappear). At least, always bleed the fish by cutting their gills. If the stream is accessible by vehicle, one solution is to have a fish box with ice waiting in the vehicle. That way, each fish can be placed in the box immediately after bleeding and gutting. In fly-in situations airplane charters or lodges may be able to help you get fish to ice quickly. If you carry beer on ice in on a day trip the problem is solved providing you drink the beer.

At the Fish House

Many recreational fishermen use commercial services to fillet, vacuum pack and freeze the fish for transport and some even remove pin bones from salmon. Other fishermen do their own packing and freezing. Regardless of who does the work, the fish should be well iced prior to processing, and processing should be accomplished as soon as possible. Delays, with whole fish sitting in melted ice water, will be disastrous to the quality of the final product.

Vacuum packing fish is ideal, and vacuum packing and freezing are also the best preparations for transporting fish by air. The vacuums should be done with enough time taken on a good machine to fully draw the vacuum. Oxygen in the air is the major cause of quality degradation, even in the freezer. For those visiting Alaska who intend to process their own fish, bringing along a good vacuum packer should be considered a high priority. Some vacuum packers are small, light and inexpensive.

One alternative to vacuum packing is to place a zip-lock bag into a tub of water to help expel the air. However, this is a poor substitute for a vacuum packer since it is much less efficient at expelling air and most plastic bags allow more air to penetrate during frozen storage than the bags made for vacuum machines. If you are not concerned about shipping weight, a better alternative is to cover the fish in salt water (2 Tablespoons to the quart) in a zip-lock bag and then expel as much air as possible from the bag.

However the fish is packed, it should be moved as quickly as possible to a freezer. The blast freezers used by most cleaning houses will freeze an afternoon catch quickly enough that it will be ready for a mid-day flight the following day. Blast freezers will bring the fish to a colder temperature than home freezers, making the fish less likely to thaw during transport.

Air Transport

Some fish cleaning houses will ship your fish to your home via Federal Express. Alternatively, they supply or sell heavy waxed cardboard boxes with insulating liners that are sized to hold 25, 50 or 100 pounds of frozen fillets to meet airline weight restrictions. These boxes will keep fish frozen in an airport--airline environment for about 24 hours at the most. Some fishermen take plastic ice chests for transporting fish. Plastic ice chests keep fish frozen only just slightly longer than the waxed cardboard boxes. Some ice chests are made for longer term storage. They are heavy, but they might be useful depending on the amount of fish and the length of the trip. If the trip has an overnight stopover, the containers of fish (cardboard box or ice chest) must find their way to a freezer for the overnight stay. If you're traveling on the same airline through your stopover, you will probably be allowed to collect the fish so that you can store them in a freezer and then check them again the next day without additional charges. Both the Seattle airport and the Anchorage airport have a commercial freezer for overnight storage in the baggage area.

On Arrival Back Home

As soon as you arrive home, place the fish into a freezer. Pieces that have partially thawed can be either used that day or the next (stored in a refrigerator), or re-frozen. If they are re-frozen, they should be separated so that they can be used first. Re-freezing partially thawed fish does degrade quality to a small degree but not enough to warrant discarding the fish. If you find some packages where the vacuum has not been drawn, use them first.

In the Kitchen

Before anything else can be done, the fish must be thawed. Vacuum packed fillets can easily be thawed in a refrigerator in about a day or in about half an hour by placing them in a sink with cold water. Using warm or hot water will ruin the fish.

Halibut fillets require very little preparation before cooking can begin. Halibut needs to have the skin and any bones removed. Also, darker parts of the fillets and discolored areas need to be trimmed away.

Salmon fillets require more detailed preparation. If the skin is going to be used in the preparation, the scales should be removed. This can be done by scraping against the direction of the scales with the back of a knife or the edge of a spoon. Doing this in a large plastic bag helps contain the scales. Most of the recipes in this book call for the skin to be removed since my family do not like the skin. For the same reason, the recipes in this book call for removal of the majority of the lateral line tissue. This tissue is the darker area that runs along the middle of the fillet next to the skin. This tissue is present in all fish but is especially prominent in salmon. The tissue is rich in nerves since the lateral line is a sense organ which detects both large and subtle water currents. The tissue has a softer texture since it is not composed of muscle, and it is easily removed with a sharp fillet knife. Leaving small amounts of the lateral line tissue is sufficient for those that prefer to not eat it. It is perfectly acceptable to leave the lateral line tissue. Removing it is an esthetic choice. Restaurants rarely remove the lateral line.

The pin bones in salmon should always be removed, except perhaps for “hot smoked” salmon, but I always remove them. Although pin bone removal is a bit tedious, the process is facilitated by tools designed for the task. Cookware shops sell a variety of tools to remove pin bones. Many look like small pliers but, unlike most hardware store pliers, the tips of the pliers touch when closed which allows a firm grasp on slender bones. Pin bone removal requires that the fillet be fully thawed. The pin bones are found in a line along the length of sections of fillet coming from above the body cavity. The tail portion of the fillet does not have pin bones. Once a few of the pin bones are removed, those that are more hidden can be found by rubbing a finger along the line of pin bones in the direction of the tail. Damage to the fillet is limited if the pin bones are pulled out along the same angle that they enter the fillet.

Fish Stock

Many of the recipes in this cookbook call for fish stock. For most fishermen the main ingredient for fish stock comes home with the catch. However, fishing tourists coming home from Alaska frequently carry home only frozen fillets since the cost of checked baggage generally is prohibitive to the transport of heads and backbones.

You may have access to heads, backbones and skin of fish from another source so I provide a general recipe for fish stock. Fresh water fish make a somewhat inferior stock but higher quality fresh water fish such as bass or crappies can be used. Most salt water fish can be used to produce a quality stock. However, avoid using salt or fresh water catfish or ling cod since their skins produce unpleasant flavors.

Halibut or salmon skin from one or two sections of fillet can be used to make wonderful stocks, so two recipes are provided for that purpose.

If you don't care to make your own stock canned fish stock or lobster stock can be purchased in the soup section of most grocery stores. Clam juice is called for in some of these recipes because of its distinctive flavor, but it should not be used as a general substitute for fish stock.

The cooked skin from fish stock is normally discarded. However, fish skin removed from stock or simply boiled in water has a special use in my kitchen. I add the skin and the water to the kibbles I feed to my dogs. The fish oils help keep their coats glossy and their appetites never lag when fish skin is on the menu. Since both cooking and freezing kill the parasites that cause salmon poisoning disease in dogs, the skin from stock made from frozen fillets is safe for them. However, it is essential to not feed dogs (or people) fresh uncooked salmon.

Basic Fish Stock

Fish stock is a basic ingredient in many of the recipes in this cookbook. Stock can be prepared ahead of time, frozen and later used in a variety of recipes. Stock can be frozen for up to three months without serious loss of quality. Thaw and warm before using. Do not salt the stock. Rather, adjust for salt in the final recipe.

Ingredients--

3 pounds of fish parts, head (gills removed), rack (internal organs removed), fins, tail and skin
1 large red onion, sliced
3 stalks of celery, coarsely sliced
1/2 bunch Italian parsley, coarsely chopped
1 inch section of fresh ginger, sliced
3 bay leaves
1 clove garlic, smashed
***10 sprigs fresh thyme,* or** 1 Tablespoon dried thyme
1 Tablespoon black peppercorns
cold water to cover
1 cup dry white wine

Procedure--

- **Combine the fish parts,** onion, celery, parsley, ginger, bay leaves, garlic, thyme and peppercorns in a large pan.
- **Cover with cold water** and heat to a simmer. Do not boil or the stock will become cloudy.
- **Simmer for 35 minutes,** stirring occasionally and skimming off the material that rises to the top.
- **Add the wine** and continue to simmer for 5 minutes.
- **Strain the stock** through a sieve or cheesecloth.
- **Use while still hot** or cool and store in glass in the refrigerator for up to a day, or cool, transfer the stock to plastic ware and freeze.

Halibut Skin Fish Stock

Halibut skin makes a wonderful stock that has the fresh taste of the ocean. It can be used in a variety of recipes as a general purpose fish stock. Thaw and warm before using. Do not salt the stock. Rather, adjust for salt in the final recipe.

Ingredients--

halibut skin from 1 or 2 sections of fillet
1/4 red onion, sliced
1 stalk of celery, coarsely sliced
3 or 4 sprigs of Italian parsley, coarsely chopped
1/8 inch slice of fresh ginger
1 bay leaf
1 clove garlic, smashed
2-3 sprigs fresh thyme
1 /2 teaspoon black peppercorns
cold water to cover
1 /4 cup dry white wine

Procedure--

- **Combine the halibut skin,** onion, celery, parsley, ginger, bay leaf, garlic, thyme and peppercorns in a large pan.
- **Cover with cold water** and heat to a simmer. Do not boil or the stock will become cloudy.
- **Simmer for 35 minutes,** stirring occasionally and skimming off the material that rises to the top.
- **Add wine** and continue to simmer for 5 additional minutes.
- **Strain the stock** through a sieve or cheesecloth.
- **Use while still hot,** or cool and store in the refrigerator for up to a day.
- **For longer storage,** cool and freeze in plastic ware. This stock may be stored frozen for 3 months with little loss of quality.

Salmon Skin Fish Stock

Salmon skin makes a stock loaded with the flavor of salmon. The skin releases enough oil, rich in omega three fatty acids, that it forms droplets on the surface of the stock. Because of its intense salmon flavor, salmon stock is best used in recipes that feature salmon. Salmon stock can also be frozen but because of the high oil content should be stored only for 2 to 4 weeks. Thaw and warm before using. Do not salt the stock. Rather, adjust for salt in the final recipe.

Ingredients--

salmon skin from 1 or 2 sections of fillet
3 or 4 sprigs of Italian parsley, coarsely chopped
1 bay leaf
2-3 sprigs fresh thyme
1 /2 teaspoon black peppercorns
2 cups cold water
1 /4 cup dry white wine

Salmon Skin Fish Stock

Procedure--

- **Combine the salmon skin,** parsley, bay leaf, thyme, and peppercorns in a pan.
- **Add cold water** and heat to a simmer. Do not boil or the stock will become cloudy.
- **Simmer for 35 minutes,** stirring occasionally, skimming off the material that rises to the top.
- **Add the wine** and continue to simmer for 5 additional minutes.
- **Strain the stock** through a sieve or cheesecloth.
- **Use while still hot** or cool and store in the refrigerator for up to a day.
- **For longer storage,** cool and freeze in plastic ware. May be stored frozen for up to 1 month.

Raw Fish -- Ceviche, Sashimi, Capriccio, Crudo, Tartar

Both salmon and halibut are excellent in raw preparations. While proper handling and processing from hook to freezer are important for all fish, they are especially important for producing sushi grade fish that is to be eaten raw. Freshly caught fish should be immediately bled, gutted and iced. Alaska's fishermen often use a club to stun or kill a freshly caught fish, or even a harpoon or gun for larger halibut. Immediately after the fish is stunned or killed, it should be bled by cutting through the gills on both sides. Next the fish should be gutted and placed on ice. Most outfitters and lodges have a supply of ice. Once iced, the fish will hold well for several hours until it can be filleted and frozen.

For fish that you intend to use for raw preparations, either clean, vacuum pack and freeze the fish yourself or arrange for priority service from a fish cleaning house.

One potential problem with eating raw fish is the parasites sometimes found in the meat. None of the many species of parasites found in raw fish can survive long when frozen. This fact has led the European Union to require that all fish served raw in restaurants be frozen first. The US Food and Drug Administration recommends freezing at a temperature of -31° F for 15 hours or at -4° F for seven days. Commercial blast freezers used by most fish cleaning services will easily meet these standards.

Mexican Style Halibut Ceviche

On the first day of our fishing holidays my group goes grocery shopping since we do our own cooking. I am always asked "did you get the ingredients for ceviche?" Later, a large piece of the first halibut we catch gets turned into ceviche. And usually, a halibut caught later in the week provides a repeat performance.

Ceviche is a preparation common to many Latin American countries in which raw fish is "cured" in the acid of citrus juice. Lime juice is used in the most classical preparations. However, lemon and white grapefruit juices also have enough acid to cure the fish. The fish will turn opaque when it is cured. The protein of the fish is altered so the fish is no longer raw. However, because the citric acid is not highly effective in killing parasites or bacteria, the dish should be made using fish that has previously been frozen, and should be carefully prepared to avoid bacterial contamination.

Halibut is perfect fish for ceviche. Ceviche should be made in the last hour or two before serving since some species of fish tend to soften with more time. Leftover halibut ceviche does not soften though, and becomes even better after a day or two in the refrigerator.

Serve on a cup of lettuce with wedges of tomato and crackers that are not heavily salted.

Mexican Style Halibut Ceviche

Ingredients--

3 medium tomatoes (skin and seeds removed*), cut into 1/2 inch squares
1 medium white onion, diced to 1/4 inch
2 cloves garlic, minced
3 Tablespoons jalapeño chilies, seeded and finely diced
3 Tablespoons Serrano chilies, seeded and finely diced
1 Tablespoon coarse salt
1 cup fresh lime juice (8 to 10 limes)
lime zest from 4 limes
3/4 cup fresh cilantro, chopped
1/4 cup extra virgin olive oil
2 pounds halibut (skin and dark areas removed), cut into about 1/2-inch squares
salt and cracked black pepper to taste

*Tomato skin can easily be removed after immersing the tomato in boiling water for about 10 seconds.

Procedure--

- **In a glass or stainless steel bowl,** mix the tomatoes, onion, garlic, jalapeño chilies, Serrano chilies, salt, lime juice, lime zest, cilantro and olive oil.
- **Add the halibut to the mixture,** pushing it down to assure all the fish is covered in the lime juice mixture.
- **Refrigerate** for at least 2 hours.
- **Season with salt and cracked black pepper to taste.**

Salmon Ceviche

Salmon ceviche is wonderful. It "cooks" more quickly than halibut ceviche so it can be served just 10 or 15 minutes after mixing. It will store for 2 or 3 days in the refrigerator but will soften somewhat during storage.

Serve the ceviche in a mound, surrounded by rings of chopped onion, chopped egg white and chopped egg yolk. Accompany with unsalted crackers as an appetizer or on a bed of watercress as a light main course.

Ingredients--

2 eggs
2 small red onions, diced to 1/4 inch pieces
1 pound salmon fillet (skin, pin bones and lateral line tissue removed), cut to 1/4 inch dice
1 cup cilantro, finely chopped
zest of 1 lime
1/2 cup lime juice, about 4 limes
2 Tablespoons capers, chopped
1/2 teaspoon Dijon mustard
1/4 teaspoon Tabasco sauce
salt and cracked black pepper to taste

Procedure--

- **Place the eggs in a steamer** and steam for 12 minutes. Cool the eggs in cold water with ice. (Steamed eggs peel much more easily than boiled eggs.)
- **Reserve 1/4 of the chopped red onions.**
- **In a glass or stainless steel bowl,** combine 3/4 of the red onions, the salmon, cilantro, lime zest and lime juice, capers, mustard and Tabasco sauce, mixing well.
- **Refrigerate** for 15 to 30 minutes.
- **Season with salt and cracked black pepper to taste.**
- **Peel the eggs** and separately chop whites and yolks.
- **Serve with onion,** egg whites and egg yolks as garnishes.

Salmon Ceviche with Dill

Classical ceviche has cilantro as its main herbal ingredient. While most people enjoy cilantro, especially in ceviche, some find the taste highly objectionable. Fortunately, the essential quality of ceviche is that it is "cooked" in the juice of high acid citrus, not that it contains cilantro. This ceviche recipe uses dill, the traditional herbal pairing for salmon. Whether or not you like ceviche with cilantro you will like it with dill. As in the preceding recipe, the salmon "cooks" quickly so may be served 10 or 15 minutes after mixing. It will store for 2 or 3 days in the refrigerator but will soften somewhat during storage.

As an appetizer, serve the ceviche in a stemmed glass with a sprig of dill as garnish along with unsalted crackers.

Salmon Ceviche with Dill

Ingredients--

1 pound salmon fillet (skin, pin bones and lateral line tissue removed), cut to 1/4 inch dice
2 small red onions, diced to 1/4 inch pieces
1 cup fresh dill, finely chopped
zest of 1 lime
1/2 cup lime juice, about 4 limes
2 Tablespoons capers, chopped
1/2 teaspoon Dijon mustard
1/4 teaspoon Tabasco sauce
salt and cracked black pepper to taste

Procedure--

- **In a glass or stainless steel bowl,** combine the salmon, red onions, dill, lime zest and juice, capers, mustard and Tabasco sauce, mixing well.
- **Refrigerate** for 15 to 30 minutes.
- **Season with salt and pepper to taste.**

Thai Style Halibut Ceviche

"Thai Style Halibut Ceviche" brings together the tastes of Mexico and Thailand. Lemon grass and kaffir lime leaves are typical of Thai food. Both Thai and Mexican cooking use cilantro and mint. And of course, both are famous for the use of chili peppers. This ceviche has enough flavors that the cilantro can be omitted for those who dislike it.

Kaffir lime leaves can be sourced in some high-end grocery stores, some Asian markets or the internet. You can also buy a kaffir lime tree on the internet which can be grown in a pot outside in the summer and brought indoors during the winter. My tree is kept in the living room during the winter and is decorated for Christmas.

Serving on a bib lettuce leaf with rice crackers accents the Thai focus.

Thai Style Halibut Ceviche

Ingredients--

1 cup lemon juice, about 7 lemons
zest of 1 lime
1/2 cup lime juice, about 4 limes
2 Tablespoons fish sauce
3 cloves garlic, minced
3 Tablespoons jalapeño chilies, seeded and chopped
2 Tablespoons fresh mint, chopped
2 Tablespoons fresh cilantro, chopped
1 lemon grass stalk, white part only, finely chopped
4 kaffir lime leaves, mid-rib removed, finely chopped
1 Tablespoon toasted sesame oil
1/4 cup extra virgin olive oil
1 pound halibut (skin and dark areas removed),
cut into about 1/2 inch squares
salt and cracked black pepper to taste

Procedure--

- **In a glass or stainless steel bowl,** mix the lemon juice, lime zest and juice, fish sauce, garlic, chilies, mint, cilantro, lemon grass, kaffir lime leaves, sesame oil and olive oil.
- **Add the halibut to the mixture,** pushing it down to assure all the fish is covered by the marinade.
- **Refrigerate** for at least 2 hours.
- **Season with salt and cracked black pepper to taste.**

Halibut Sashimi Bowl with Lime Ginger Sauce

Sashimi is raw fish cut into bite sized pieces. Uniform size and shape are distinctive of the sashimi presentation. This sashimi can be used as a main course. Reducing portion size makes a nice appetizer.

Serve with "Sushi Rice" (Page 146) and *"Lime Ginger Sashimi Sauce" (Page 153).*

Ingredients--

"Sushi Rice" (Page 146)
halibut fillet, 4 ounces per portion (skin and dark areas removed), cut into pieces 1/4 inch thick, 1 inch wide and 2 inches long
1 green onion per serving, sliced

Procedure--

- **Prepare serving bowls** by adding 3/4 cup of sushi rice, sliced green onions and halibut.
- **Serve the sauce to the side** to be added to the dish according to individual preference or spread 4 Tablespoons of the sauce over each portion.

Salmon Carpaccio

Carpaccio is a method of preparation used in Italian cooking. It involves taking sections of raw meat or fish, pounding them thin with a mallet and serving them with lemon, olive oil, salt and pepper.

Serve as an appetizer with unsalted crackers or toasted brown bread.

Ingredients --

1 pound salmon fillet
(skin, pin bones and lateral line tissue removed)
4 Tablespoons extra virgin olive oil
1 cup watercress greens
zest and juice from 1 lemon
salt and cracked black pepper to taste

Procedure--

- **Slice the fillet into sections** about 2 in x 2 in x 1/2 in.
- **Brush olive oil** on both sides of each section, place each section between sheets of waxed or parchment paper and gently flatten the fish with a kitchen mallet until it is about 1/4 inch thick.
- **Spread the watercress over a serving plate,** place the salmon over the greens and refrigerate until serving.
- **Whisk together the remaining olive oil,** zest and lemon juice, salt and pepper, and drizzle over the carpaccio just prior to serving.

Salmon Crudo

Crudo is the Italian version of sashimi. It differs from carpaccio by being cut thin rather than being pounded thin.

Serve salt to the side in individual salt cellars to provide an elegant presentation.

Ingredients --

1 pound salmon fillet (pin bones, skin and lateral line tissue removed)
3 Tablespoons extra virgin olive oil
2 lemons, quartered
1 cup fresh basil leaves, *coarsely chopped*
sea salt

Procedure--

- **Wrap the salmon in plastic wrap** and place in a freezer until quite firm but not frozen. This will allow cutting very thin slices.
- **With a very sharp knife,** cut the salmon across the grain into thin (1/8 inch) slices.
- **Drizzle the olive oil on serving plates,** place the salmon crudo on the oil and garnish with the lemon quarters and basil leaves.
- **Serve salt to the side.**

Salmon Tartare

Tartare is a European style of preparing raw beef, horse or fish. The meat is mixed with spices and herbs and served as an appetizer. If you like raw fish in sushi, you will definitely like salmon tartare.

Serve in lettuce cups garnished with cherry tomatoes and accompany with unsalted crackers.

Ingredients --

1 pound salmon fillet (pin bones, skin and lateral line tissue removed)
4 Tablespoons shallots, finely chopped
2 Tablespoons fresh dill, finely chopped
2 Tablespoons fresh chives, finely chopped
2 Tablespoons extra virgin olive oil
juice from 1 lemon
salt, cracked black pepper and Tabasco sauce to taste

Procedure--

- **Mince the salmon** to about 1/8 inch cubes.
- **Mix well with the remaining ingredients** just prior to serving.

Halibut Tartare

Halibut brings its special fresh taste to this tartare. It is a wonderful appetizer for a light summer meal.

Belgian endive leaves heaped with halibut tartare and garnished with slices of cherry tomatoes make a nice presentation.

Ingredients --

1 pound halibut fillet (skin, and any dark areas removed)
4 Tablespoons shallots, finely chopped
3 Tablespoons red bell pepper, finely chopped
2 Tablespoons capers, finely chopped
2 Tablespoons fresh dill, finely chopped
2 Tablespoons extra virgin olive oil
juice from 1 lime
salt, cracked black pepper and Tabasco sauce to taste

Procedure--

- **Mince the halibut** to about 1/8 inch cubes.
- **Mix well** with the remaining ingredients just prior to serving.

Smoked and Salt Cured Fish

This section contains three methods for producing smoked and salt cured fish. Both halibut and salmon are superb when smoked. Smoked fish is a delicious product which can be eaten by itself and which greatly increases the diversity of dishes that can be prepared from the catch of a successful fishing trip. Since smoked fish can be eaten without additional preparation, it also makes an excellent gift and always finds its way into the bags of food treats that I give friends at the holidays.

Smoking fish requires a home smoker. While prices are varied, you will probably find that even the least expensive models will produce excellent results and will last for years. Most of these smokers are designed specifically for "hot process" smoking. The fish is first soaked in brine solution and then cooked for a long time at low temperature while also being smoked.

Many species of wood are available on the market as chips for use in smoking. Alder is the traditional wood for smoking fish in the Pacific Northwest. Apple, cherry, hickory, and mesquite are also commonly available. Maple is excellent but not commonly sold. Some of these woods produce mild smoke and others produce a stronger smoke. My own favorites are maple and cherry.

I have successfully smoked salmon for years using both the "hot smoked" and "cold smoked" methods. When I brought home a large volume of halibut for the first time I wondered if it could be smoked with the same success I had previously enjoyed with salmon. I quickly discovered that "hot smoked" halibut is as wonderful as "hot smoked" salmon, even though the smoke does not penetrate throughout halibut as it does with salmon.

Fish can also be preserved by curing it in salt. Salt curing is a common procedure for salmon in many northern European countries and results in "gravlox", a product that is similar to "cold smoked" salmon, except that it lacks the flavor of smoke. However, I do not recommend halibut for either the "cold smoked" or the "gravlax" processes.

Hot Smoked Fish

This procedure is suitable for many species of fish but is especially designed for salmon and halibut. The product is a smoked fish that is typical of the Pacific Northwest.

Ingredients--

2 inch wide piece of fish fillets (For salmon, skin on but pin bones removed. For halibut, skin removed)
1 cup rock or kosher salt
1 cup dark brown sugar
1 cup soy sauce
about 3 quarts water
cooking oil to coat smoker racks
about 1 quart wood chips

Procedure--

- **Prior to smoking,** the fish must be brined. To make the brine, place the salt, brown sugar, soy sauce and water in a non-reactive bowl (glass or stainless steel). Stir to dissolve ingredients.
- **Add the fish and refrigerate** between 8 to 14 hours.
- **Transfer the fish to oiled smoker racks** and allow to air dry for about 1/2 hour. Discard the brine.
- **Turn on the smoker in an outdoor location,** place racks of fish in the smoker and load the smoke source with wood chips. Smoke for 3 to 4 hours. Refill the smoke source and smoke for an additional 2 to 4 hours. When the surface of the fish looks dry and smoked, check the inner texture by breaking open a piece. Timing will vary according to the thickness of the fish and the outside temperature. The fish should be firm, well-cooked but moist inside and should easily separate into flakes. The internal temperature will be about 145° F.
- **Remove the racks of fish** from the smoker. Cool and remove the fish from the racks.
- **Refrigerate after cooking.** Before serving, remove the skin and grey lateral line tissue from salmon. The lateral line tissue tastes fine but its color and soft texture are unappetizing to many people. The fish will store well in refrigeration for 7 to 14 days.

Cold Smoked Salmon

This is an excellent version of the smoked salmon that is served as the "lox" of "lox and bagels". While the salmon is smoked, it is also preserved by light salting. Making it yourself yields a product which has a brighter, fresher taste than commercial products.

Cold smoked salmon should be refrigerated and eaten within two to three days since, unlike commercial products, it is not pasteurized.

Ingredients--

about 1 quart wood chips
sections of salmon fillets 8 to 10 inches long
(skin on but with pin bones removed)
ice cubes
about 1/2 cup rock or kosher salt
6 to 10 sprigs of fresh dill

Procedure--

- **Fire up the smoker** and wait until it is producing a good volume of smoke.
- **Place ice cubes into a heat proof pan,** almost filling it.
- **Place the salmon,** skin side down, on the ice cubes.
- **Place the pan in the smoker** as far from the heat source as possible and smoke for 30 minutes.
- **Remove the salmon from the smoker** and place on a sheet of plastic kitchen wrap.
- **Coat the salmon** with a thin layer of rock salt.
- **Add a layer of dill sprigs** and wrap with the plastic wrap.
- **Place the wrapped bundle in a pan,** place a board on the fish and a 1-pound weight on the board.
- **Refrigerate for 1 day.**
- **Remove, unwrap,** add a second layer of salt over the dill and refrigerate for a second day.
- **Remove the salmon** from the wrapped package, discard the dill, rinse briefly in cold water, and pat dry with a paper towel.
- **Slice thinly and serve.**

Gravlox

This salt cured salmon is the centerpiece of the Swedish smörgåsbord. *It is similar to cold smoked salmon but saltier and the flavor of dill is more intense. This process produces a firm product. If you prefer a lighter texture, use a shorter curing time and less weight.*

*Serve with brown bread or toasted bagel halves, cream cheese and condiments; chopped fresh dill, finely chopped red onion, capers and finely chopped boiled egg as an appetizer. Traditionally, it is served with "*hovmästarsås*" ("Mustard Dill Sauce") (Page 154) and simple boiled potatoes and ice cold vodka or aquavit.*

As with "Cold Smoked Salmon" gravlox should be stored in a refrigerator. Because of the heavier salting it will remain fresh for four or five days.

Ingredients--

1/2 cup of rock salt
1/2 cup dark brown sugar
2 pieces of salmon fillet, each about 10 inches long
(skin on but pin bones removed)
6 Tablespoons aquavit or vodka
1 Tablespoon dill seed
large bunch of fresh dill, large stems removed

Procedure--

- **Mix the salt and sugar.**
- **Place a sheet of plastic wrap** in a glass or ceramic baking dish.
- **Place 1 salmon fillet** skin side down on the plastic; sprinkle with aquavit or vodka, cover well with half the salt-sugar mixture and cover with the dill seed and the fresh dill.
- **Sprinkle the second salmon fillet** with aquavit or vodka and cover with the remainder of the salt and sugar mixture, patting it in so that it will stay in place.
- **Lay the second fillet** on top of the dill, skin side up.
- **Wrap the plastic wrap tightly** around the fish, place a board or a plate over the fish and place about 3 to 4 pounds of weight on the plate. Cans of food or a clean rock will work as a weight.
- **Refrigerate** for 2-1/2 days turning the bundle about every 12 hours.
- **Remove the fish from the bundle,** rinse to remove the dill and any remaining salt and pat dry.
- **Cut very thin slices** on the bias to produce slices that are wider than the fillet is thick.

Recipes using Smoked Fish

Smoked fish is a wonderful product in its own right. In fact, it is so good that some people will only eat it unadulterated by other tastes. Others will concede that sometimes smoked fish could be used in simple ways such as on a toasted bagel with cream cheese and perhaps a bit of dill, capers and red onion. On the other hand, having smoked salmon provides a gateway to a myriad of more complex recipes that include smoked fish as an ingredient. This section contains a few such recipes.

Smoked Salmon Pâté or Dip

This easy to make pâté is a crowd pleasing appetizer. When I ask friends what can I bring to their dinner parties the answer is often "Oh, the salmon pâté please!"

Prepare one to seven days before serving. Use block cream cheese for a pâté texture or whipped cream cheese for the texture of a dip.

To serve, place about 1/2 Tablespoon of pâté on rounds of cucumber or small pieces of toasted dark bread and top with a small sprig of dill. Or, serve the pâté in a serving dish with cucumber rounds and toast in separate dishes. For a smörgåsbord *appetizer of prepared salmon products provide dishes of "pâté", "Hot Smoked Salmon" (Page 33), "Gravlox" (Page 37), finely chopped red onion, finely chopped dill, small capers, cream cheese and lemon slices. Let guests prepare their own small open-faced sandwiches with various combinations of these ingredients. In Scandinavia, it is traditional to serve small glasses of ice cold vodka or aquavit with a* smörgåsbord.

Smoked Salmon Pâté or Dip

Ingredients--

8 oz "Hot Smoked" salmon, skin removed
4 oz cream cheese
juice of 1/2 lemon
3 Tablespoons fresh dill, thick stems removed
1 Tablespoon Worcestershire sauce
salt to taste

Procedure--

- **Place 6 ounces of salmon,** the cream cheese, lemon juice, dill and Worcestershire sauce into a food processer. Pulse until the mixture is smooth.
- **Season with salt to taste,** pulsing to blend.
- **Place 2 ounces of salmon into the processer** and pulse 1 or 2 times to leave small chunks of salmon in the mixture.

Mac and Cheese with Smoked Salmon

This may be the ultimate mac and cheese. This recipe uses white cheddar cheese. I prefer "Cougar Gold" from the dairy store at Washington State University. It is excellent, can be ordered for mail delivery except in summer and ships well since it is made in a sealed can. However, it does need to be stored in a refrigerator.

This can be made using broiled salmon with 2 teaspoons of added salt to produce a dish with a lighter flavor. Serve with a green salad, perhaps lettuce, tomato and cucumber and a non-cheese dressing.

Ingredients--

1/2 pound elbow macaroni
6 Tablespoons unsalted butter
3 Tablespoons flour
3 cups milk
1/2 cup yellow onion, finely diced
1/2 teaspoon nutmeg, ground
1 Tablespoon white pepper, ground
1 large egg, beaten
12 ounces sharp white cheddar cheese, grated
10 ounces "Hot Smoked" salmon (Page 33), flaked
1 cup panko bread crumbs

Procedure--

- **Preheat an oven to 350^0 F.**
- **Cook the macaroni** in boiling water according to package directions until al dente, drain and reserve.
- **As the macaroni is cooking,** place 3 Tablespoons of butter and the flour in a pan and cook while continually whisking for 3 minutes.
- **Add the milk,** onion, nutmeg and white pepper and continue to whisk until the mixture is thick.
- **Remove from heat.** Slowly add the egg, whisking continually.
- **Whisk in 8 ounces** of cheese until melted.
- **Place the mixture** into a 2-quart buttered baking dish.
- **Fold in the cooked macaroni** and salmon.
- **Melt 3 Tablespoons of butter** and coat the bread crumbs.
- **Sprinkle 4 ounces of cheese** and the bread crumbs over the macaroni mixture.
- **Bake for 30 minutes,** covering the dish if it browns too quickly.
- **Remove from the oven** and rest the dish for 5 minutes, allowing it to become more firm.

...almon with Fettuccine in ...n Cream Sauce

I make this dish with packaged pasta on the first day of each Alaskan fishing trip with the thought that it motivates my friends to fish harder. Both fettuccini and smaller shapes such as shells or bows work well.

However, since handmade pasta is wonderful and worth the effort, for those that care to try, I provide this recipe for handmade fettuccini. It requires a pasta machine to form the dough into thin sheets that are cut to form noodles. The ability to make handmade pasta opens a seemingly endless cornucopia of culinary possibilities to a home chef.

The pasta is added to the sauce pan as the "Parmesan Cream Sauce with Smoked Salmon" (Page 155) is being made.

Smoked halibut can also be used and will produce a more delicate dish. This dish shines with only a simple green salad with a light dressing. I use an "Orange Pecan Salad" (Page 147) with "Orange Honey Salad Dressing" (Page 156).

Smoked Salmon with Fettuccine

Ingredients-- *(for four servings)*

2 cups of unbleached flour
2 large eggs
1 teaspoon salt
perhaps a few Tablespoons water

Procedure--

> *Traditional recipes call for placing the flour and salt onto a flat surface, making a well in the middle, breaking the eggs into the well and mixing the eggs into the flour. I let my food processer do the work.*

- **Process the eggs, salt and flour** until the dough is formed into a ball. Toward the end of processing it may be necessary to add water, a few drops at a time, before the machine can form the dough into a ball.
- **Remove the dough,** form it into lemon sized balls, coat them with flour, cover with a dish cloth and allow them to rest for 10 minutes.
- **Prepare a place to dry the sheets of pasta.** Spread kitchen towels or a bed sheet on a table or other large surface.
- **Assemble the pasta machine.**
- **Working with lemon sized balls of dough,** roll the dough through the largest setting of the machine. Dust with flour; fold the piece double and roll, dust

and double until the dough's surface has a silken feel. Then, without folding, roll the dough sequentially through thinner and thinner machine settings, dusting with flour as needed to retain the silken texture.

- **After starting the sheet in the machine,** turn the roller with one hand and catch the sheet coming from the machine with the other hand.
- **After rolling the dough through the thinnest setting,** place the sheet on the drying area.
- **Repeat with the remaining dough.**
- **Turn the sheets every 10 minutes** until they are dry enough to cut and still maintain their shape as noodles. The sheets will feel like soft leather.
- **Boil about 4 quarts of water.**
- **Cut the sheets into pieces** about 12 inches long. Cut the noodles on the pasta machine, allowing the noodles to fall onto a floured plate.
- **Melt the butter in a large frying pan** in the first step of the sauce preparation.
- **Add the noodles** to the boiling water, and then remove them as soon as they rise to the top. This takes only seconds.
- **Drain the noodles and immediately add them to the melted butter** as the second step of sauce preparation.
- **Finish the "Parmesan Cream Sauce with Smoked Salmon"** (155).

Smoked Salmon Cheesecake

Many Louisiana restaurants offer savory crawfish cheesecake as an appetizer, a tradition that is the inspiration of this cheesecake.

Serve in a pool of "Meunière Sauce" (Page 157) and garnish with diced tomato, peeled and seeded, and minced chives. Serve as a first course or as main course with steamed asparagus, a green salad with sliced strawberries with "Honey Orange Salad Dressing" (Page 156) and a sparkling white wine.

Ingredients--

2 cups butter crackers, crushed
1 egg white, yolk reserved
9 Tablespoons unsalted butter
3 packages (24 ounces total) cream cheese
1/2 cup sour cream
1/8 teaspoon paprika
1/8 teaspoon cracked black pepper
1/8 teaspoon cayenne pepper
1/8 teaspoon garlic powder
1 teaspoon salt
juice of 1/2 lemon
3 eggs plus 1 egg yolk
1 pound "Hot Smoked" salmon (skin, pin bones and lateral line tissue removed), crumbled

Procedure--

- **Cook the eggs by steaming them for 12 minutes.** Place them in cold water with ice to cool.
- **Coarsely chop the iceberg lettuce,** arugula and romaine lettuce. Mix and place on serving plates.
- **Peel, seed and coarsely chop the tomatoes** and reserve.
- **Flake the smoked salmon** and reserve.
- **Cut the chicken into a 1/2 inch dice** and reserve.
- **Peel and coarsely chop the boiled eggs** and reserve.
- **Peel, seed and coarsely chop the avocado,** sprinkle with lemon juice to prevent browning and reserve.
- **Crumble the blue cheese** and reserve.
- **Finely chop the chives,** and mix with coarsely chopped watercress, thicker stems removed and reserve.
- **Arrange each reserved ingredient** as a row over the lettuce mixture.
- **Drizzle the dressing over the salad.**

Potato Salad with Sour Cr[illegible]
Chives and Smoked Fish

> *This salad, served on lettuce leaves accomp[illegible]ied by a dish of salted sliced fresh ripe tomatoes, makes a wonderful brunch. If it is served as a side to a meal that has fish as the main course it can be made without the smoked fish.*

Ingredients--

2 pounds of small red potatoes
3/4 cup sour cream
1/4 cup plain yogurt
1/3 cup of fresh chives, chopped
8 ounces of "Hot Smoked" fish (salmon or halibut) (Page 33), flaked
1/2 cup shallots, finely chopped
2 teaspoons salt
1 teaspoon cracked black pepper

Procedure--

- **Boil the potatoes** in a large pot of salted water until fork tender. Drain and cool.
- **Cut the potatoes** to bite sized pieces and toss with the sour cream, yogurt, chives, fish, shallots, salt and pepper.

Chowders, Stews and Bisques

Nothing is quite as satisfying on a cold winter day as hearty fish soup. A bowl of chowder or bisque accompanied by a crispy artisan bread, unsalted butter, a simple green salad and perhaps a glass of good ale made with cascade hops in the Pacific Northwest (or in your own kitchen*) is simple enough to make after work and stylish enough to serve guests on Sunday. While the range of fish stews, chowders and bisques is enormous, the recipes that follow are designed for the stars of this cookbook, salmon and halibut.

*Making your own beer is a very satisfying hobby. Home brews can surpass the quality of market brews at a fraction of the cost.

Pacific Northwestern Halibu Chowder

New England clam chowder is an East Coast classic which has now become popular throughout the country. Using halibut makes this rich creamy chowder special to the Pacific Northwest. Ideal for a cold winter day, this chowder makes a complete meal when served with oyster crackers or French bread, unsalted butter and a green salad.

Ingredients--

3 slices *bacon,* diced
1 cup red onion, 1/4 inch dice
3 cups red potatoes peeled and diced to 1/2 inch cubes
1 bottle (8 ounces) clam juice
14 to 16 ounces halibut (skin and dark areas removed), cut to about 1/2 inch cubes
3 Tablespoons flour
1 cup milk
2 cups half-and-half cream
salt, cracked black pepper and Tabasco sauce to taste

Procedure--

- **Cook the bacon** in a heavy saucepan.
- **Remove the bacon** to a paper towel to drain and reserve.
- **Sauté the onion in the bacon drippings** until translucent.
- **Add the potatoes** and clam juice, and simmer until the potatoes are almost tender, about 10 minutes.
- **Add the halibut** and simmer about 5 minutes.
- **Whisk the flour** into 1/2 cup of the milk until smooth and then add it and the remaining milk and cream to the potato-halibut mixture.
- **While continuing to stir,** cook over medium heat until the chowder thickens.
- **Remove from heat.**
- **Chop the reserved bacon** and add it to the chowder.
- **Season with salt, cracked black pepper and Tabasco sauce to taste.**

New England Halibut Chow

While "Pacific Northwestern Halibut Chowder" (Page 53) is fashioned after the basic New England clam chowder recipe, this recipe is both richer and flavored with herbs that compliment the flavor of the halibut.

Oyster crackers or good bread and unsalted butter with a green salad complete the meal.

Ingredients--

6 Tablespoons unsalted butter
3 Tablespoons flour
1 cup red onion, chopped
3 cups red potatoes, peeled and diced to 1/2 inch cubes
1 bottle (8 ounces) clam juice
14-16 ounces halibut (skin and dark areas removed), cut to about 1/2 inch cubes
1 cup milk
2 cups half-and-half cream
2 Tablespoons fresh thyme, leaves removed from stem, chopped
1 teaspoon fresh rosemary, leaves removed from stem, finely chopped
salt and cracked black pepper to taste

Procedure--

- **Combine 3 Tablespoons of butter** and the flour in small saucepan.
- **While constantly whisking,** heat on high until the mixture turns light brown. Remove from heat and reserve.
- **Sauté the onion** in 3 Tablespoons of butter until translucent.
- **Add the potatoes** and clam juice, and simmer until the potatoes are almost tender, about 10 minutes.
- **Add the halibut** and simmer about 5 minutes.
- **Add the milk,** cream and reserved butter flour mixture.
- **While continuing to stir,** cook over medium heat until the chowder thickens.
- **Remove from heat.**
- **Add the thyme and rosemary.**
- **Season with salt and pepper to taste.**

Smoked Salmon Cheesecake

Procedure--

- **Pre-heat an oven to 275°.**
- **Mix the cracker crumbs,** egg white and 2 Tablespoons of butter thoroughly.
- **Coat a 10 inch spring form pan** with 1 Tablespoon of butter.
- **Place the cracker mixture** on the bottom of the spring form pan and press down well.
- **Bake for 8 minutes** and remove from the oven.
- **In a mixer or food processor,** mix 6 Tablespoons of butter, the cream cheese, sour cream, paprika, black pepper, cayenne pepper, garlic powder, salt, lemon juice, eggs and egg yolk.
- **Fold in the salmon** and place the mixture in the spring form pan.
- **Bake at 275° for 1 hour.** Turn the oven off and leave the cheesecake in the oven for 1 hour without opening the oven.
- **Remove from the oven** and let cool for 2 hours. Cut into serving portions.

Cobb Salad with Smok

Cobb salad is a classic American dish c
the Brown Derby Restaurant in Los Ang
California in 1937. While the traditional ...ipe calls for bits of crisp bacon the flavor of smoked salmon is a superb, and to my taste, a superior substitute.

Serve with "Cobb Salad Dressing" (Page 158).

Ingredients--

3 eggs, hard boiled and peeled
1/2 head iceberg lettuce, about 4 cups
1 bunch arugula, about 2 cups
1/2 head romaine lettuce, about 2-1/2 cups
2 medium tomatoes, peeled and seeded
2 cups of "Hot Smoked" salmon, flaked
2 breasts of chicken, poached, broiled or grilled
1 avocado
2 Tablespoons lemon juice
1/2 cup blue cheese
2 tablespoons chives
1 bunch watercress

Manhattan Halibut Chowder

With the addition of bacon and tomatoes, Manhattan chowder takes the concept of chowder in a very different direction. But who can argue with a direction flavored with bacon and garden fresh tomatoes.

Like other chowders, it is a complete meal when served with good bread and butter and a green salad.

Ingredients--

6 slices bacon, diced
1 cup red onion, 1/4 inch dice
2 cloves of garlic, minced
1 cup celery, 1/4 inch dice
4 bottles (32 ounces total) clam juice or fish stock
8 ounces tomato sauce
2 bay leaves
3 cups red potatoes, washed and unpeeled, 1/2 inch dice
2 pounds fresh tomatoes,
skin and seeds removed and finely chopped
14 -16 ounces halibut (skin and dark areas removed),
cut to about 1/2 inch cubes
2 Tablespoons fresh thyme,
leaves removed from stem and chopped
1/2 cup fresh parsley,
leaves removed from stem and chopped
salt and cracked black pepper to taste

Procedure--

- **In a large heavy pan,** cook the bacon and reserve.
- **Sauté the onions,** garlic and celery in the bacon drippings until the onion is translucent.
- **Add the clam juice,** tomato sauce, bay leaves and potatoes. Simmer until the potatoes are almost tender, about 10 minutes.
- **Add the tomatoes** and simmer about 5 minutes.
- **Add the halibut** and simmer until the halibut is opaque, about 5 minutes.
- **Remove from the heat.**
- **Crumble the reserved bacon** and add to the chowder.
- **Add the thyme and parsley.**
- **Season with salt and pepper to taste.**

Thai Style Salmon Chowder

Salmon is ideal in this fusion of North American and Thai classics. Tom Yum, Thailand's most famous soup, features shrimp in a flavorful broth. American chowders feature potatoes in a rich broth. This soup has elements of both with the salmon taking the starring role. Eight ounces of peeled shrimp could be added to reinforce the fusion concept.

Continue the Asian theme by serving a salad with lettuce, green onions and diced mango or papaya dressed with "Orange Honey Salad Dressing" (Page 156). Mango juice could be substituted for the orange juice in the dressing.

Thai Style Salmon Chowder

Ingredients--

2 large red potatoes, peeled and cut to pieces about 1-inch square
2 medium carrots, peeled and cut to 1-inch lengths
3 cups "Salmon Skin Fish Stock" (Page 14)
1-1/2 cups coconut milk
2 Tablespoons fresh ginger, grated
lemon grass, 3 two-inch lengths of white stalk, grated
1 teaspoon chili-garlic paste
3 cups of fresh button mushrooms, sliced
1 1/2 pounds of salmon (skin, pin bones and lateral line removed), cut into about 1 inch by 2 inch sections
2 green onions, sliced into 1/4 inch sections
2 medium tomatoes cut into wedges
salt to taste

Procedure--

- **Boil the potatoes and carrots** in fish stock until they can be partially pierced with a fork.
- **Continue boiling** and add the coconut milk, ginger, lemon grass and chili-garlic paste.
- **When the potatoes are nearly fork tender** reduce to a simmer and add the salmon and mushrooms.
- **When the salmon has cooked through,** remove from heat, add the green onions and tomatoes.
- **Season with chili-garlic paste and salt to taste.**

Holiday Salmon and Oyster Stew

I originally developed this recipe for a light meal during the winter holidays. Using cream rather than milk adds some holiday richness, but milk may be substituted. The addition of salmon expands the complexity of flavor and makes the stew heartier. If you omit the oysters, add more salmon.

Serve with oyster crackers or rustic bread with unsalted butter and a light green salad tossed with lemon juice, olive oil, salt and pepper.

Ingredients--

1 cup celery, 1/4 inch dice
1 cup shallots, 1/4 inch dice
4 Tablespoons unsalted butter
1 cup clam juice or fish stock
3 cups half and half cream
1 pound salmon fillet (skin, pin bones and lateral line removed), cut into about 1 inch cubes
1 pint fresh small oysters, shucked, including liquid
2 Tablespoons fresh thyme, finely minced
salt, cracked black pepper and cayenne pepper to taste

Procedure--

- **Sauté the celery and shallots** in butter until the shallots become translucent.
- **Add the clam juice and cream,** bring the mixture to a simmer but do not boil.
- **Add the salmon** and simmer until the outer half has cooked and the interior is still raw.
- **Add the oysters** and continue to simmer until the salmon is cooked through and the oysters are just cooked.
- **Add the thyme.**
- **Season with salt, black and cayenne peppers to taste.**
- **Serve immediately** to preserve the tenderness of the oysters.

Salmon Chowder with Fennel

Salmon with a hint of fennel produces flavorful and rich chowder with a light licorice flavor.

Serve with French bread, unsalted butter and a green salad with lettuce, shaved fennel bulb, shaved parmesan cheese, sliced red onion and tangerine segments; dressed with a mixture of 1/2 cup white balsamic vinegar, 1/4 cup olive oil, salt, cracked black pepper and 1 teaspoon ground cumin seeds.

Salmon Chowder with Fennel

Ingredients--

2 large red potatoes, peeled
and cut into pieces abut 1-1/2 inches square
1 large red onion, cut into 1 inch cubes
4 cups rich stock (duck or beef)
1 fifteen ounce can diced tomatoes
1-1/2 cups frozen white corn
chili-garlic paste and salt to taste
3 pounds salmon (skin, pin bones and lateral line removed),
cut into about 1-1/2 inch by 1-1/2 inch sections
4 cups fennel leaves, chopped

Procedure--

- **Boil the potatoes** and onion in the stock until the potatoes are tender.
- **Add the tomatoes** and corn.
- **Season with chili-garlic paste** and salt to taste.
- **Add the salmon** and simmer until the salmon is cooked, about 3 minutes.
- **Stir in the fennel and serve.**

Halibut Bisque

Halibut is perfect for producing classic, thick, creamy bisque. Although it uses a variety of ingredients, this bisques' prominent flavor is the distinctive fresh ocean flavor of halibut.

Although excellent as a soup course for a larger meal, this bisque is filling enough to serve as a main course accompanied by a green salad, crusty bread and unsalted butter.

Ingredients --

7 Tablespoons unsalted butter
4 Tablespoons extra virgin olive oil
1 cup red onion, 1/4 inch
1 cup carrots, 1/4 inch dice
1 cup celery, 1/4 inch dice
1 clove garlic, minced
1 cup Italian parsley leaves, coarsely chopped
4 Tablespoons fresh thyme leaves, finely chopped
3 Tablespoons flour
1 cup heavy cream
***4* cups "Halibut Skin Stock"** (Page 12)
3 pounds halibut (skin and dark areas removed), cut to 1 inch cubes
Salt, ground white pepper and Tabasco sauce to taste
1 ounce brandy

Procedure --

- **Melt 4 Tablespoons of butter and the oil** and sauté the onion, carrots, celery, garlic, parsley and thyme until the onions are translucent.
- **In a separate pot,** melt 3 Tablespoons of butter, add the flour and cook while continually whisking until the mixture foams, making a very light colored roux.
- **Add the cream to the roux** and continue to whisk over medium heat until the mixture thickens, making a white sauce.
- **Add the white sauce,** stock and halibut to the vegetable mixture and cook until the fish is opaque throughout, about 4-5 minutes.
- **Using a food processor,** blender or emersion blender, process the mixture until smooth. Some small particles will remain which can be removed with a fine sieve if desired.
- **Reheat the bisque** and season with salt, pepper and Tabasco sauce to taste.
- **Add brandy just prior to serving.**

Salmon Bisque

This rich creamy soup has an intense salmon flavor. It is ideal as either a first course or as a main course rounded out with country bread, unsalted butter and a green salad.

Ingredients--

3 pounds salmon fillet (skin, pin bones and lateral line tissue removed), 2 pounds cut to 1 to 1-1/2 inch cubes, 1 pound cut to 1/4 inch cubes
1-1/2 cups "Salmon Skin Stock" (page 14)
1-1/2 cups white wine
2 medium tomatoes, peeled, seeded and coarsely chopped
3 Tablespoons unsalted butter
3 Tablespoons flour
2 cups half-and-half cream
salt and ground white pepper to taste

Salmon Bisque

Procedure--

- **Simmer the coarse cut salmon** in the stock and white wine for 10 minutes.
- **Add the tomatoes** and simmer for 2 minutes.
- **Process the mixture** in a blender or food processor and reserve.
- **Heat the butter until melted,** add the flour and whisk until the mixture foams, making a very light colored roux.
- **Add the cream to the roux** and whisk continually until the cream sauce thickens. Remove from heat and reserve.
- **Return the reserved salmon mixture to a pan** and bring to a simmer.
- **Add the fine cut salmon to the salmon mixture** and simmer for 2 minutes.
- **Add the reserved cream sauce to the salmon mixture** and heat well.
- **Season with salt and white pepper to taste.**

Salmon Preparations

Salmon is a wonderfully versatile fish that can be prepared in an endless number of ways. This section presents several kinds of preparations, expanding the range offered by the sections on smoked fish, raw fish, chowders, burgers and grilling.

Numerous methods for pan-broiling are offered. The majority of these recipes require only a short preparation time, making them especially useful for producing wonderful meals quickly after a busy day.

Pan-broiled salmon is best when skin and pin bones are removed. Skin can be removed from pieces of fillet with a sharp fillet knife. Hold one corner edge of the skin on a cutting board and slide the knife between the meat and the skin. Pin bones are objectionable to most diners but they can easily be removed using fish bone tweezers. Several different styles of fish bone tweezers are available in kitchen and cooking stores. Hardware pliers are not suitable for removing pin bones since the tips do not touch when closed.

Some people dislike the color and texture of the lateral line that runs along the side of the fish just inside the skin. The lateral line is a sense organ that is rich in nerves. A sharp fillet knife can be used to remove the majority of the tissue.

Basic Pan-Broiled Salmon

This simple preparation allows the salmon to shine on its own. It should be served with accompaniments that do not upstage it, such as "Cucumber Tarragon Sauce" (Page 159), mashed potatoes dressed with unsalted butter, salt and black pepper and steamed broccoli dressed with lemon juice, salt and pepper.

Ingredients--

2 to 3 Tablespoons unsalted butter
juice of 1 lemon
four 2 inch wide sections of salmon fillet (skin, pin bones and lateral line removed)
1/4 teaspoon salt
1/4 teaspoon cracked black pepper

Procedure--

- **Pre-heat a broiler to 400° F.**
- **Melt the butter in an oven-safe frying pan.**
- **Add the lemon juice** to the butter.
- **Place the salmon into the pan,** season with salt and pepper and baste with the butter lemon mixture.
- **Broil and baste with the pan juices** every 2 minutes until the salmon is cooked through (8 to 12 minutes) and slightly browned.

Pan-Broiled Salmon Encrusted with Basil Pesto

The fame of basil pesto is richly deserved. Pesto made from basil fresh from the garden is perfect for dressing pasta, pizza or home grown tomatoes. However, it may be even better as a topping for broiled salmon.

Served with a savory green salad featuring ripe tomatoes, French bread, unsalted butter and a bottle of cold white wine from the Pacific Northwest, this is a perfect meal to celebrate summer.

Ingredients--

1/2 cup pine nuts, toasted
2 packed cups fresh basil leaves
2 cloves garlic
2/3 cup extra virgin olive oil
1/2 teaspoon salt
1/2 cup freshly grated parmesan cheese
salt and cracked black pepper to taste
2 Tablespoons unsalted butter
four 2-inch wide sections of salmon fillet
(skin, pin bones and lateral line removed)

Procedure--

- **Toast the pine nuts.** Spread the nuts in a single layer on a microwave-safe plate and microwave on high for 2 minutes. Stir and repeat until the nuts are toasted to a light brown color.
- **Combine the basil,** garlic, pine nuts and olive oil in a food processor and pulse until the mixture is smooth.
- **Add the parmesan cheese** and pulse until the cheese is in small identifiable bits.
- **Season with salt and pepper to taste** and reserve.
- **Pre-heat a broiler to 400° F.**
- **Melt the butter in an oven-safe frying pan.**
- **Place the salmon into the pan** and broil until lightly brown and flaky, about 10 minutes.
- **Coat the salmon with the reserved pesto** and return to the broiler for 1 minute.

Pan-Broiled Salmon Encrusted with Sliced Almonds

An almond coating brings both a uniquely satisfying flavor combination and a pleasing contrast of textures. This preparation is well worth the small amount of extra effort. The result is fabulous. The printer who produced the draft copies of this cookbook for editing reported "It's rich but so good!"

Use "Lemon Butter Sauce" (Page 160) to dress both the salmon and mashed potatoes, and serve with steamed snow peas or asparagus.

Ingredients--

1/3 cup sliced almonds
four 2-inch wide sections of salmon fillet
(skin, pin bones and lateral line removed)
1/4 teaspoon salt
1/4 teaspoon cracked black pepper
4 Tablespoons flour
1 egg, beaten
2 Tablespoons unsalted butter

Pan-Broiled Salmon Encrusted with Sliced Almonds

Procedure--

- **Pre-heat a broiler to 400° F.**
- **Spread the almonds** on a plate.
- **Season the fillet sections** with salt and pepper.
- **Place the flour** and beaten eggs in separate bowls.
- **Press one surface of fillet sections** into the flour, then press the flour coated surface into the egg. Press the egg coated surface into the almonds, coating the entire surface.
- **Melt the butter in an oven-safe frying pan.**
- **Place the salmon almond side down** into the pan and sauté about 1 minute.
- **Turn the salmon almond side up** and broil until the almonds are lightly browned and the fish is cooked, about 8 to 9 minutes. Cover with a lid or aluminum foil if the almonds brown too quickly.

Pan-Broiled Salmon Encrusted with Pecans and Honey

This preparation brings flavors and textures that enrich and compliment the flavor of the salmon. Using fireweed honey brings the dish a Pacific Northwest flavor, but any other lightly flavored high quality varietal honey, such as sourwood or clover, also works well.

Ingredients--

3/4 cup pecans, crushed to pieces 1/4 to 1/8 inch
3 Tablespoons honey
2 Tablespoons unsalted butter
four 2 inch wide sections of salmon fillet
(skin, pin bones and lateral line removed)
1/4 teaspoon salt
1/4 teaspoon cracked black pepper

Procedure--

- **Combine the pecans and honey.**
- **Pre-heat a broiler to 400° F.**
- **Melt the butter in an oven-safe frying pan.**
- **Place the salmon into the pan,** season with salt and pepper and broil for 8 minutes.
- **Coat the salmon** with the pecan honey mixture and return to the broiler for 2 to 3 minutes until the pecans are toasted.

Pan-Broiled Salmon with Key Lime and Honey

The unique flavor of Key limes combines with the flavor of a mild honey (fireweed, sourwood or clover) to produce a broiled salmon that is both delicate and flavorful. Mashed potatoes and spinach sautéed in olive oil with salt and pepper and finished with 4 Tablespoons of heavy cream work nicely as side dishes.

Ingredients--

Zest and juice of 3 Key limes
3 Tablespoons honey
2 Tablespoons unsalted butter
4 two-inch wide sections of salmon fillet
(skin, pin bones and lateral line removed)
1/4 teaspoon salt
1/4 teaspoon cracked black pepper

Procedure--

- **Pre-heat a broiler to 400° F.**
- **Combine the lime zest,** juice and honey.
- **Melt the butter in an oven-safe frying pan.**
- **Season the salmon with salt and pepper,** place into the pan and baste with the honey lime mixture.
- **Broil and baste with pan juices** every 2 minutes until the salmon is cooked through (about 7 to 10 minutes).

Pan-Broiled Salmon with Thyme, Garlic, Lemon and Butter

This preparation is simple, easy and very flavorful. My tasters assure me that the amount of garlic is "just right".

For a quick and easy meal, serve with "Rice with Green Peas and Toasted Pecans" (Page 148) and a simple green salad.

Ingredients--

4 Tablespoons unsalted butter
2 Tablespoons garlic, minced
4 Tablespoons lemon juice
2 Tablespoons fresh thyme leaves
2 Tablespoons extra virgin olive oil
four 8-ounce pieces of salmon fillet (skin, pin bones and lateral line removed)

Procedure--

- **Pre-heat a broiler to 400^0 F.**
- **Melt the butter** and add the garlic, lemon juice, chili-garlic paste and thyme leaves to make a sauce.
- **Coat the bottom of an oven-safe frying pan** with olive oil.
- **Place the salmon in the pan,** pour the sauce over the salmon and broil until lightly brown and flaky.
- **Baste with the sauce about every 2 minutes** until done (about 7 to 10 minutes).

Adriatic Pan-Broiled Salmon

This recipe is a modification of a very memorable fish dish I had in a restaurant on the Adriatic Coast of Italy. It has the essence of southern Italy, only better since it's salmon!

Ingredients--

4 Tablespoons extra virgin olive oil
four 8-ounce pieces of salmon fillet
(skin, pin bones and lateral line removed)
zest and juice of 1 lemon
2 Tablespoons fresh rosemary, chopped very fine
20 Kalamata (Greek black) olives, pitted
1/4 teaspoon salt
1/4 teaspoon cracked black pepper

Procedure--

- **Pre-heat a broiler to 400^0 F.**
- **Coat the bottom of an oven-safe frying pan** with olive oil.
- **Place the salmon into the pan** and season with the lemon zest, rosemary, pepper and salt.
- **Pour the lemon juice over the salmon** and add the olives to the pan.
- **Broil until the fish is lightly brown** and flaky.
- **Baste with the pan drippings** about every 2 minutes until done (about 10 to 12 minutes).

Pan-Broiled Salmon with Maple Glaze and Toasted Pecans

I was asked to make this dish for a birthday dinner after not making it for two years. I rediscovered that it is both easy and crowd-pleasingly delicious.

Ingredients--

1/4 cup pecans, toasted and crushed
1/2 cup real maple syrup
2 Tablespoons fresh garlic, minced
4 Tablespoons soy sauce
2 Tablespoons unsalted butter
four 8-ounce pieces of salmon fillet
(skin, lateral line and pin removed)
1/4 teaspoon cracked black pepper

Procedure--

- **Pre-heat a broiler to 400^0 F.**
- **Toast pecans** in a microwave on high for 4 minutes.
- **Cool pecans,** then crush or chop to 1/4-inch pieces.
- **Mix the maple syrup,** garlic and soy sauce.
- **Melt the butter in an over-safe frying pan.**
- **Place the salmon in the pan**, season with black pepper, pour maple syrup sauce over salmon and broil until lightly brown and flaky. Baste with sauce every 2 minutes until done (about 10 to 12 minutes).
- **Sprinkle the salmon** with the pecan pieces at serving.

Spinach and Salmon Soufflé

Made with either "Hot Smoked" salmon (Page 33) or "Basic- Pan Broiled Salmon" (Page 71), this light soufflé makes a wonderful Sunday brunch.

Serve with a light garden salad with mixed greens, tomato, green onions and cucumber dressed with balsamic vinegar, olive oil, salt and pepper, accompanied by a sparkling white wine.

Ingredients--

2 (10-ounce) packages frozen chopped spinach
1/4 cup unsalted butter
1/4 cup flour
2 cups milk
1/2 teaspoon salt
1/8 teaspoon ground white pepper
1/4 teaspoon grated nutmeg
6 egg yolks, beaten
1/2 cup freshly grated Parmesan cheese
8 egg whites
1/4 teaspoon cream of tartar
8-10 ounces broiled or smoked salmon, flaked

Procedure--

- **Cook the spinach** according to package directions, drain, cool and reserve.
- **Pre-heat an oven to 350° F.**
- **Place the butter and flour** in a pan and cook while continually whisking for about 3 minutes until the mixture foams, making a very light roux.
- **Add the milk,** salt, pepper and nutmeg and continue to whisk until the mixture is thick.
- **Slowly add the egg yolks,** whisking continually.
- **Remove from heat** and whisk in the cheese until melted.
- **Fold in the reserved spinach**.
- **Beat the egg whites with cream of tartar** until they are stiff.
- **Fold 1/3 of the egg whites** into the spinach mixture.
- **Fold in the salmon** and the remainder of the egg whites.
- **Transfer the mixture** to an 8-cup buttered soufflé dish and bake at 350° F for 45 minutes.

Asian Poached Salmon

This salmon with Asian flavors is perfect for a light meal. After cooking the salmon, strain the broth, take two cups of the clear broth and reduce to 1 cup. Thicken with 2 Tablespoons of butter and serve over white rice with a green vegetable to the side of the poached salmon. Or, place "Sushi Rice" (Page 146) in a bowl, sauce the rice and serve the fish on top.

Ingredients--

1 cup white wine
1 cup fish stock (Page 10)
1/2 cup soy sauce
1/2 cup hoisin sauce
1 Tablespoon chili-garlic paste
2 Tablespoons lemon grass, white part only, finely chopped
4 Tablespoons red onions, finely chopped
2 Tablespoons kaffir lime leaf, chopped (sources page 24)
1 Tablespoon black peppercorns
four to six 2-inch wide sections of salmon fillet
(skin and pin bones removed)

Procedure--

- **In a large saucepan combine the wine,** fish stock, soy sauce, hoisin sauce, chili-garlic paste, lemon grass, onions, kaffir lime leaf, and peppercorns and bring to a simmer.
- **Slide the fish fillets** into the simmering broth and cook until the fish flakes.

Salmon Mousse Ravioli in Cream Sauce

If salmon were native to Italy, Italians would absolutely make this dish. Of course, making ravioli means making pasta. This recipe is worth the effort.

Three to five ravioli per person make an excellent appetizer. As a main course serve 10 to 12 per person accompanied by steamed asparagus, or a salad of greens, fresh grapefruit sections and toasted pecans dressed with "Orange Honey Salad Dressing" (Page 156), substituting grapefruit juice for the orange juice.

Ingredients--

homemade pasta, rolled into sheets (Page 44)
10 – 12 ounces of salmon (skin and pin bones removed), cut into 2-inch pieces
1/2 teaspoon salt
4 dashes of Tabasco sauce
2 to 4 Tablespoons and then 3/4 cup heavy cream
egg white from 1 egg
3 Tablespoons unsalted butter
1 cup freshly grated Parmesan cheese
1/4 teaspoon freshly grated nutmeg

Salmon Mousse Ravioli in Cream Sauce

Procedure--

- **Prepare the pasta,** rolling it into wide sheets (Page 45).
- **Pulse the salmon,** salt and Tabasco sauce in a food processor until the mixture is smooth.
- **Add 1 Tablespoon of cream and pulse,** adding more cream as needed to produce a thick paste.
- **Cut 2-1/2 inch squares from the pasta sheets.** Put 2 teaspoons of mousse onto a pasta square and cover with a second square, removing as much air as possible and sealing edges after brushing with a small amount of egg white. Dust with flour to prevent sticking after forming.
- **Melt the butter in a large frying pan.**
- **Place the ravioli into a large pot of boiling water** and cook until they float to the top, about 1 minute.
- **Drain the ravioli** with a strainer and place them into the frying pan with the melted butter.
- **Add the cream and heat** until the cream has thickened.
- **Add the parmesan cheese,** gently mix until the cheese is melted, and dust lightly with grated nutmeg when the ravioli are plated.

Salmon Pinwheels

These pinwheels make a flavorful plate of appetizers for a group of 4 to 6 people. Garnish with sprigs of parsley or cilantro.

Ingredients--

8 ounces salmon (skin, lateral line and pin bones removed), grilled or broiled, then flaked
8 ounces brick cream cheese
1/4 cup tomato salsa
1/4 cup fresh parsley, chopped
1-1/2 teaspoons ground cumin
1 large flour tortilla

(Or, substitute green salsa for tomato salsa and chopped cilantro for parsley.)

Procedure--

- **With a spoon, blend the salmon,** cream cheese, salsa, parsley and cumin enough that the salmon flakes are about 1/2 inch pieces.
- **Spread the mixture on a tortilla,** bringing some to the very edge.
- **Roll the tortilla into a cylinder** and cut into 3/4 inch rounds.

Salmon Loaf with Cucumber Tarragon Sauce

This home-style salmon loaf makes a great dinner with leftovers that can be used to make excellent sandwiches.

Serve with "Cucumber Tarragon Sauce" (Page 159), baked potato dressed with unsalted butter, salt and pepper or "Cucumber Tarragon Sauce," and mixed lettuce dressed with oil, lemon juice, salt and pepper.

Ingredients--

2 pounds salmon (skin and pin bones removed)
1/2 cup mayonnaise
1 cup panco bread crumbs
2 Tablespoons fresh tarragon, finely chopped
2 eggs, beaten
2 teaspoons salt
2 teaspoons cracked black pepper
1 Tablespoon smoked paprika
1 Tablespoon unsalted butter

Procedure--

- **Pre-heat an oven to 350^0 F.**
- **Finely mince 1/2 pound of salmon.**
- **Dice the remaining 1-1/2 pounds of salmon into 1/8 to 1/4-inch pieces.**
- **Mix the salmon,** mayonnaise, bread crumbs, tarragon, eggs, salt and pepper.
- **Butter a large loaf pan** and place the salmon mixture into the pan, patting down gently to smooth the top.
- **Sprinkle the salmon loaf with paprika.**
- **Bake at 350^0 F for 45 minutes.**

Poached Salmon Salad

Salmon salad is lighter and far more flavorful than the more common tuna salad. It is equally good as a salad at an elegant brunch served with sparkling white wine or in a sandwich in a school lunch.

For a salad, serve heaped on a bed of chopped watercress surrounded by chopped tomatoes that have been peeled and seeded. For a sandwich, dress with sliced tomatoes and romaine lettuce. Or, serve as an appetizer with lavasch or another unsalted cracker.

Ingredients--

1 cup Riesling wine
1 cup water
1 cup white balsamic vinegar
1 Tablespoon black peppercorns
2 sprigs fresh rosemary
1 pound salmon (skin and pin bones removed), cut into 2-inch sections
1/2 cup celery, cut into 1/4-inch pieces
3 Tablespoons fresh dill, chopped
3 Tablespoons shallots, finely diced
1 Tablespoon capers, chopped
2 teaspoons lemon juice
1/2 teaspoon Tabasco sauce
1/3 cup mayonnaise
1/2 teaspoon salt

Procedure--

- **Bring a mixture of wine,** water, vinegar, black peppercorns and rosemary to a simmer.
- **Poach the salmon** in the wine mixture for 7 to 10 minutes until it flakes.
- **Remove the salmon** from the poaching liquid, cool, pat dry and separate into flakes, breaking them into pieces about 1 inch square.
- **Mix the flaked salmon,** celery, dill, shallots, capers, lemon juice, Tabasco sauce, mayonnaise and salt.

Salmon Stuffed with Crab Meat

This version of salmon stuffed with crab is based on methods used to stuff flounder on the Gulf Coast, a dish that has been popular for decades.

Serve with "Refried Potatoes" (Page 150) and a spinach salad with candied walnuts, strawberries, bits of goat cheese and a dressing made with 1/3 cup of balsamic vinegar, 1/3 cup of olive oil, salt and cracked black pepper to taste.

Ingredients--

4 Tablespoons green bell pepper, 1/4-inch dice
2 cloves garlic, minced
1/2 cup yellow onion, 1/4-inch dice
1/4 cup unsalted butter
1 teaspoon dry ground yellow mustard
1/2 teaspoon cayenne pepper
1/2 teaspoon salt
1/2 cup panko bread crumbs
3/4 pint lump crab meat
3 Tablespoons mayonnaise
4 sections of salmon fillet (skin, pin bones and lateral line removed), trimmed into 5 to 5-1/2 inch squares, 3/4 inch thick
1/2 cup salmon trimmings, chopped to 1/4-inch pieces
1/4 cup extra virgin olive oil
1/4 teaspoon cracked black pepper

Procedure--

- **Sauté the green pepper,** garlic and onion in the butter until the onion is translucent and cool mixture.
- **Add the mustard,** cayenne pepper, salt, bread crumbs, crab meat, mayonnaise, and salmon trimmings to the sautéed mixture.
- **Gently toss to blend** the crab mixture.
- **Pre-heat a broiler to 400^0 F.**
- **Cut a slit** along the grain in the middle of each salmon fillet, leaving 1 inch uncut at top and bottom.
- **Fold the edges of the fillet sections up** and pin the edges together with toothpicks to form a pocket in the center.
- **Coat the bottom of a baking sheet** with olive oil.
- **Place the salmon pockets on the baking sheet** and season with salt and pepper.
- **Spoon the crab mixture into the salmon pockets** and press lightly to firm the mixture.
- **Broil the stuffed fillets** until the stuffing is lightly browned and the salmon is cooked through.

New Orleans Style Barbecued Salmon Strips

Shrimp and grits are a tasty southern tradition for Sunday brunch. Here is a variation that uses salmon. There are no messy tails to pull off and the flavor of the salmon enhanced by the spices is delicious.

Although the salmon and "Barbecue Sauce" (Page 161) can be served with mashed potatoes they are designed to go with "Cheesy Creamy Grits" (Page 151).

Ingredients--

3 Tablespoons unsalted butter, melted
1-1/2 pounds salmon fillet (skin, pin bones and lateral line removed), cut across the grain to strips about 3/4 inch by 3 to 4 inches
1/2 teaspoon salt
1/2 teaspoon cracked black pepper
1 teaspoon onion powder
4 Tablespoons fresh parsley, finely chopped

Procedure--

- **Pre-heat a broiler to 400^{0} F.**
- **Melt the butter** in a small sauce pan on medium heat.
- **Place the salmon in a bowl,** season with salt, pepper and onion powder and toss with the melted butter.
- **Place the salmon on a broiler pan** and broil, without turning, until the top is just slightly brown.
- **Place the salmon on "Creamy Cheesy Grits"** or mashed potatoes and ladle "Barbecue Sauce" (Page 161) over the dish.
- **Garnish with parsley.**

Thai Style Salmon Stir Fry

Salmon is perfect for stir frying. The salmon holds its shape well and its taste is a perfect match with mixed vegetables. The oranges are unusual but add a refreshing depth of flavor and texture.

The cooking goes quickly so it is important to have all ingredients pre-cut and ready to add to the pan. Traditionally stir frying is done in a wok, but a large non-stick frying pan works well.

Ingredients--

3/4 cup coconut milk
2 Tablespoons honey
2 cups orange juice
2 Tablespoons corn starch
1/2 cup extra virgin olive oil
1 Tablespoon lemon grass, white part only, chopped very fine
2 cloves garlic, minced
2 Tablespoons chili-garlic paste
2 Tablespoons fresh ginger, *grated*
1 cup green bell pepper, cut to 1/2 inch squares
1 cup red onion, diced to 1/2 inch pieces
2 pounds salmon (pin bones, skin and lateral line removed), cut to 1-inch cubes
1 cup fresh basil, preferably Thai, very coarsely chopped
salt and cracked black pepper to taste
2 medium sweet oranges or tangerines, segments separated
1/3 cup dry roasted peanuts
1/3 cup coconut flakes

Thai Style Salmon Stir Fry

Procedure--

- **Stir the coconut milk** and honey together.
- **Divide the orange juice** into two cups and stir the cornstarch into one of the cups, mixing well.
- **Heat the olive oil in a large pan** or wok and add the lemon grass, garlic, chili-garlic paste and ginger. Sauté on high heat for 20 seconds.
- **Add the bell pepper and onion** and sauté for 1 minute.
- **Add the salmon** and sauté for 3 minutes, adding more oil if necessary.
- **Add the orange juice** and sauté for 2 minutes.
- **Add the orange juice with corn starch** and coconut milk-honey mixture and stir the liquids until thickened.
- **Continue cooking until the salmon** is just cooked through.
- **Stir in the basil.**
- **Season with salt and pepper to taste.**
- **Serve on individual plates,** garnished with the orange segments, peanuts and coconut.

Halibut Preparations

Halibut is the finest white-fleshed fish the ocean has to offer. The meat has its own special characteristics. It has a mild flavor reminiscent of the ocean. Since it has a low fat content it will not have any trace of a "fishy" taste that some people find objectionable in other fish.

Halibut will not brown when grilled or broiled without a coating. Cook halibut only until it is opaque throughout, flakes and is still moist (145° F). Halibut that is coated in batter or crumbs of some sort and then broiled or fried will more easily retain moisture and be flakey and tender even if cooked a bit longer than absolutely necessary.

Halibut is ideal as an addition to stews (Pages 52-68) and other braised preparations such as "Halibut Etouffée" (Page 110) since it will not fall apart as easily as other fish and will remain tender. Halibut is also ideal for Ceviche ("Mexican Style Halibut Ceviche", Page 18 or "Thai Style Ceviche", Page 24) since the pieces will hold their shape even if the ceviche is stored for a day or so.

Halibut fillets require very little preparation prior to cooking. Halibut skin, which should always be removed, can be used to make an excellent "Halibut Skin Fish Stock" (Page 12). Some cuts of fillet may have a few bones that should be removed. Also, some parts of fillets may have a dark color. These areas should be removed but can be added to the skin for preparation of stock. Remaining pieces should be clear of any stain or discoloration and be white with a slight translucence. An ideal thickness for cooking is usually one inch. Regardless of cooking method, this thickness will take about 10 minutes to cook. Reducing a large piece of halibut to portions by cutting across the grain results in pieces that will flake very easily when cooked.

Halibut cheeks are a special treat and one of the finest of the ocean's delicacies. They deserve to be reserved for a special occasion and given a special preparation such as "Halibut Cheeks stuffed with Tarragon Salmon Mousse" (Page 106).

Pan-Broiled Halibut

This basic preparation has only the clear clean taste of halibut that is perfectly balanced with the complex flavors of "Fig Chutney" (Page 170).

Ingredients--

6 eight-ounce pieces of halibut, skin removed
2 Tablespoons unsalted butter
1 teaspoon salt
1 teaspoon cracked black pepper

Procedure--

- **Pre-heat a broiler to 400°F.**
- **Remove the skin from the halibut** and cut it into serving-sized portions.
- **Melt the butter in an oven safe-frying pan.** The fish has very little fat content so having the fish in some butter while broiling is best.
- **Place the halibut pieces into the pan,** turning them to coat both sides with butter.
- **Season with salt and pepper.**
- **Place the pan under the broiler** and broil 10 to 12 minutes until the fish will separate in flakes with a fork. It will brown very little.

Tropical Halibut

Halibut lends itself brilliantly to braising. Braising in the mixture of tropical flavors presented here creates a wonderfully flavorful dish that is perfect served over steamed rice (Page 148).

Serve with a simple steamed green vegetable such as snow peas sprinkled with the juice of the 1/2 lime remaining from preparing the halibut.

Ingredients--

12 ounces sweetened coconut flakes, toasted
1 cup pine nuts, toasted
1 fifteen ounce can unsweetened coconut milk
1 Tablespoon chili-garlic paste
zest and juice of 1/2 lime
2 Tablespoons grated fresh ginger
1-1/2 cups fresh pineapple, cut to about 1/2 inch cubes
1 large orange, sectioned and cut in 1/2 inch pieces
3/4 cup basil, coarsely chopped
3 Tablespoons unsalted butter
six 2-inch by 7-inch sections of halibut fillet, 1-1/2 inches thick (skin removed)
1 teaspoon salt
1 teaspoon cracked black pepper

Procedure--

- **Toast the coconut flakes.** Place the flakes on a microwaveable plate, and microwave for 1 minute. Stir. Repeat until the flakes are lightly browned.
- **Toast the pine nuts** using the same toasting process.
- **Pre-heat a broiler to 400° F.**
- **Make a sauce by mixing the coconut milk,** chili-garlic paste, lime zest and juice, ginger, 3/4 of the pineapple, 1/3 of the orange, 3/4 of the coconut flakes, 3/4 of the pine nuts and 3/4 of the basil.
- **Add 1 cup of the sauce** to the remainder of the pineapple, orange and basil, and reserve.
- **Reserve the unused coconut flakes** and pine nuts.
- **Melt the butter in an oven-safe baking dish.**
- **Place the halibut pieces in the dish.**
- **Season the halibut with salt and pepper.**
- **Pour the sauce over the halibut,** place the pan under the broiler and broil 12 to 15 min until the fish flakes with a fork.
- **Serve the fish over white rice** with sauce over both.
- **Garnish with the reserved mixture** and the reserved coconut and pine nuts.

Rosemary Grilled Skewers of Halibut

Grilling halibut requires a delicate touch. By the time the fish browns slightly it is overdone. The trick is to remove the fish from the heat just as it becomes cooked through (145° F). Using rosemary skewers makes an appealing presentation.

For a grilled theme meal, serve with mixed grilled vegetables (tomatoes, green and yellow summer squash, eggplant, asparagus and bell peppers).

Ingredients--

3 Tablespoons fresh rosemary,
chopped finely in a food processor
2 teaspoons salt
1 teaspoon cracked black pepper
1 cup extra virgin olive oil
1 pound halibut (skin and dark areas removed),
cut into 1-1/2 cubes
36 medium button mushrooms, about 1-1/2 inches diameter
36 large cherry tomatoes
36 chunks of red onion, about 1-1/2 inches wide
12 sprigs of rosemary with woody stems, about 12 inches long
or bamboo skewers, soaked in water

Procedure--

- **Mix the rosemary,** salt, pepper and olive oil to make a marinade.
- **Soak the halibut in the marinade** between 8 and 24 hours.
- **Prepare the skewers** with alternating pieces of halibut, mushroom, tomato and onion.
- **Return the filled skewers to the marinade.**
- **Prepare the grill with medium hot coals** and spray or brush the grate with oil.
- **Place the skewers on the grill** and brush them with the remaining marinade as they cook.
- **Cook for 3 to 4 minutes** per side until the fish will flake with a fork or is 145° F.

Halibut Pot Pie

This is comfort food at its best. Based on chicken pot pie this halibut version brings out the best of halibut. The halibut is tender, juicy and flavorful. Salmon can be used with equal success.

Ingredients--

1 package frozen puff pastry
2 cups "Halibut Skin Fish Stock" (Page 12) or, if using salmon "Salmon Skin Fish Stock" (Page 14)
2 cups white wine
1 Tablespoon salt
1/2 cup of shallots, thinly sliced
10 to 12 springs of fresh thyme
1-1/2 pounds of halibut (skin and dark areas removed) cut into 1-inch cubes (if using salmon remove skin, pin bones and lateral line)
1 pound small red potatoes, cut into quarters
3 medium carrots, cut into diagonal 1/4-inch rounds
3 ribs of celery, cut into diagonal 1/4-inch sections
1 cup frozen peas
4 Tablespoons unsalted butter
4 Tablespoons flour
2 cups milk
4 Tablespoons fresh thyme leaves, chopped
1 teaspoon freshly ground nutmeg
salt and cracked black pepper to taste
unsalted butter to coat individual soufflé dishes or pie pan
1 egg, beaten

Procedure--

- **Set the puff pastry out to thaw.**
- **Combine the fish stock,** wine, salt, shallots and sprigs of thyme and bring to a simmer.
- **Add the fish** and poach until opaque.
- **Remove and reserve the fish.**
- **Strain and reserve the broth.**
- **Boil the potatoes** in salted water until fork tender.
- **Steam the carrots until partly cooked,** add the celery and peas and continue steaming until cooked.
- **Pre-heat an oven to 350° F.**
- **Melt the butter,** add the flour and whisk until the mixture foams, forming a very light roux.
- **Add 3 cups of the poaching broth and the milk,** cook on high heat until thickened.
- **Remove from heat** and season with the thyme, nutmeg and salt and pepper to taste.
- **Add the fish,** potatoes, carrots, peas and celery.
- **Butter 8 one-cup individual soufflé dishes.**
- **Spoon the mixture** into the soufflé dishes.
- **Cut rounds of puff pastry** and cover the dishes, pressing the edge of the pastry to the dishes. Brush the top with egg white and pierce the top with a sharp knife to provide a vent.
- **Place the dishes on a baking sheet** to catch overflow and bake at 350° F until the pastry is puffed, golden brown and cooked through, about 25 minutes.

Halibut Cheeks Stuffed with Tarragon Salmon Mousse

Halibut cheeks are considered by some to be the finest food to come from the sea. They deserve a special preparation. This one brings together the best of Alaskan fish-- halibut cheeks and salmon. The dish can also be made with serving-sized pieces of regular halibut. Serve with "Tarragon Hollandaise Sauce" (Page 163). The tarragon pairs wonderfully with the taste of halibut. Mashed potatoes (with some of the hollandaise sauce) and steamed green peas or asparagus with a drizzle of lemon juice are easy and elegant accompaniments.

Tarragon Salmon Mousse

Ingredients--

10 – 12 ounces of salmon, (skin and pin bones removed) cut into 2-inch pieces
1/2 teaspoon salt
4 dashes of Tabasco sauce
1 to 2 ounces heavy cream
3 heaping Tablespoons fresh tarragon leaves

Procedure--

- **In a food processor,** pulse the salmon, salt and Tabasco sauce to a paste, add cream and tarragon and pulse until smooth.

Stuffed Halibut Cheeks

Ingredients--

4 large halibut cheeks or 4 portions of halibut, (skin removed) 3 by 3 inches
"Tarragon Salmon Mousse"
2 Tablespoons unsalted butter
1/2 teaspoon salt
1 Tablespoon flour

Procedure--

- **Cut slits into the side of the halibut cheeks** or cut slits into portions of the halibut to about 1/2 inch from the bottom and the sides.
- **Stuff mousse into the slits,** using as much as possible.
- **Salt the fish** and dust with a fine coating of flour.
- **Turn a broiler on high.**
- **Melt the butter in an oven-safe frying pan,** and sauté both sides of the fish for 30 seconds.
- **Cover the pan** and place under the broiler until the fish almost flakes. Remove the cover and finish under the broiler until the fish flakes and is a bit brown.
- **Sauce with "Tarragon Hollandaise Sauce"** (Page 163).

Fish Tacos with Beer Batter Deep Fried Halibut

Halibut is superbly moist and flakey when beer battered. It goes perfectly in West Coast-style tacos, my son's favorite halibut dish.

To serve on tacos, first fry flour tortillas by sprinkling a few drops of olive oil on a hot pan and fry briefly until a few brown spots appear.

Serve the tacos with shredded cabbage, ripe avocado slices and "White Taco Sauce for Fish Tacos" (Page 164). One pound of halibut will make eight 10 inch tacos. The beer battered fried halibut also can be served with "Tartar Sauce" (Page 165) or on a bun with lettuce, tomato and one of two the sauces.

Fish Tacos with Beer Batter Deep Fried Halibut

Ingredients--

cooking oil for deep fryer
1 cup flour
2 Tablespoons cornstarch
1 teaspoon baking powder
1/2 teaspoon salt
1 egg
1 cup India pale ale with Cascade hops
1 pound halibut (skin removed),
cut into 1-inch by 1-inch by 3-inch pieces
1 teaspoon salt
1 teaspoon cracked black pepper

Procedure--

- **Heat cooking oil in a fryer to 370° F.**
- **Mix the flour,** cornstarch, baking powder, salt and egg together in a mixing bowl.
- **Just prior to cooking** add the ale to a mixing bowl and mix until most of the lumps are gone.
- **Season the halibut with salt and pepper.**
- **Coat the halibut pieces in batter** and deep fry until the coating is golden brown and the fish flakes, about seven minutes.
- **Drain on paper towels** and serve.

Halibut Etouffée

Etouffée is one of South Louisiana's signature dishes. Halibuts' firm texture is ideal for this preparation. Etouffée is served on a bed of steamed rice (Page 148) which dilutes the spice intensity. As written, this dish is quite spicy. However, to produce a moderately spicy etouffée, reduce the amount of the peppers by half. Prepare and measure all ingredients prior to cooking since the ingredients will be added quickly.

Crispy French bread with unsalted butter and a simple green salad complete the meal.

Ingredients--

4 Tablespoons of peanut oil
4 Tablespoons flour
3/4 cups white onions, 1/2-inch dice
3/4 cups green bell pepper, 1/2-inch dice
3/4 cup celery, 1/2-inch dice
3 cups "Halibut Skin Stock" (Page 12)
1 teaspoon salt
2 teaspoons cayenne pepper
2 teaspoons ground white pepper
2 teaspoons cracked black pepper
1 Tablespoon fresh basil, chopped
1-1/2 teaspoon fresh thyme leaves, chopped
1/2 cup tomato paste
1/3 pound unsalted butter
2 pounds halibut (skin removed), cut into 1-inch cubes
1 cup green onions, both white and green parts, chopped

Procedure--

- **Make a dark roux in a heavy pan,** preferably iron. Heat the peanut oil, add the flour and with a long-handled whisk, continually stir until the mixture becomes a chocolate-colored roux. Be sure to scrape the bottom of the pan to keep the roux from scorching. (This is best done on high heat, but **be careful to avoid splashing the roux on your hand**).
- **Reduce heat to medium;** add the onions, bell pepper, celery and 1 cup of stock. Continue to whisk and cook until the onions are transparent.
- **Add the salt,** cayenne pepper, white pepper, black pepper, basil, thyme leaves, 1 cup of stock and the tomato paste. Stir with a wooden spoon.
- **Cook until the vegetables are soft.** Adjust the thickness to a thick gravy with remaining stock.
- **Add the butter and fold in the halibut** until it is covered by the mixture. Cook until the halibut is cooked through.
- **Remove from heat; serve on steamed rice** (Page 148) and top with the green onions when serving.

Pan Fried Halibut with Two Sauces

This dish is a great choice for a dinner party. Most fish can be pan fried and this method produces a wonderful result.

Serve individually with a piece of halibut on a pool of 3 to 4 Tablespoons of "Meunière Sauce" (Page 157) and top the halibut with 1 to 2 Tablespoons of "Pecan Butter Sauce" (Page 166). It is not necessary to use the two sauces but they put the 'party' in "dinner party".

"Refried Potatoes" (Page 150) and steamed snap peas sprinkled with lemon juice complete the plating.

Ingredients--

2 eggs, beaten
1/2 cup milk
1/4 teaspoon Tabasco sauce
1 cup flour
1/2 teaspoon salt
1/2 teaspoon cracked black pepper
1/2 teaspoon cayenne pepper
1/2 teaspoon dried oregano
peanut oil
6 six ounce portions of halibut (skin removed)

Procedure--

- **Beat the eggs with the milk** and Tabasco sauce and reserve.
- **Mix the flour,** salt, black pepper, cayenne pepper, and oregano and reserve.
- **Heat enough peanut oil** to come halfway up the sides of the fillets to about 350^0 in a frying pan.
- **Coat the fish with the flour mixture,** shake off the excess, dip in the egg mixture and dip again in the flour mixture.
- **Without crowding,** fry the fish on one side until golden brown, turn and fry the other side.
- **Drain on paper towels.**
- **To serve,** place a piece of fish on a pool 4 to 5 Tablespoons of "Meunière Sauce" (Page 157) and top with a Tablespoon of "Pecan Butter Sauce" (Page 166).

Pan Roasted Halibut

Pan roasting is an ideal method for preparing halibut since it results in a halibut that is moist, flaky and nicely browned.

It can be served with any of the sauces in the sauce section but is especially good with "Fish Velouté Sauce with White Wine and Tarragon" (Page 167).

Ingredients--

4 Tablespoons flour
1 teaspoon cayenne pepper
2 teaspoons salt
4 six ounce portions of halibut (skin and dark areas removed)
1 teaspoon cracked black pepper
4 Tablespoons extra virgin olive oil

Procedure--

- **Mix the flour,** cayenne pepper, 1 teaspoon salt, and reserve.
- **Pre-heat an oven to 350^0.**
- **Season the halibut** with salt and black pepper and coat with flour mixture.
- **Heat the oil in an oven-safe frying pan** and sauté the halibut on both sides until browned.
- **Cover the pan** and bake for 10 minutes.

Yakutat Halibut Nuggets

This is a southern salute to the source of all the halibut. Coating fish in corn flour is a southern tradition. If you have difficulty finding corn flour, some brands of "fish fry" only contain corn flour.

Using small pieces of deep fried halibut gives bites of fish that are great served with "Honey Mustard Sauce" (Page 168) as a "Kid's Meal", as an appetizer, or on salad greens as a light main course salad.

Ingredients--

peanut oil
1 to 2 pounds halibut (skin and dark areas removed), cut into 1-inch cubes
Tabasco sauce
salt
cracked black pepper
1 to 2 eggs, beaten
corn flour or corn meal (enough to coat the fish)

Procedure--

- **Heat 1-1/2 inches of oil to 350° F** in a deep pan or fryer.
- **Sprinkle the fish with Tabasco sauce,** salt and pepper.
- **Dip pieces of the fish individually into the egg,** then coat with corn flour.
- **Fry a few pieces of fish** at a time until golden brown, drain and serve.

Halibut Almandine

New Orleans restaurants have served trout almandine for over a century using speckled sea trout (greater weak fish). Substituting halibut makes this classic recipe even better.

Mashed potatoes and steamed asparagus sprinkled with lemon juice are nice compliments to the fish.

Ingredients--

4 six-ounce pieces of halibut (skin and dark areas removed)
2 cups milk
2 teaspoons Tabasco sauce
2 teaspoons salt
1 cup flour
1 teaspoon ground white pepper
3/4 cup unsalted butter
2 tablespoons canola oil
1/2 cup sliced almonds
2 Tablespoons lemon juice
2 teaspoons Worcestershire sauce
1/4 cup parsley, chopped

Procedure--

- **Soak the halibut for 30 minutes in a mixture of the milk,** Tabasco sauce and 1 teaspoon salt.
- **Season the flour** with 1 teaspoon of the salt and the white pepper.
- **Bring 1/4 cup of butter** and the oil to a simmer.
- **Remove the halibut from the milk,** pat dry and dredge in the seasoned flour, shaking off the excess.
- **Fry the halibut** in the butter and oil mixture until golden brown on both sides.
- **As the fish is frying,** sauté the almonds in 1/2 cup of melted butter until lightly browned to make an almond butter sauce.
- **Remove the almond butter sauce from the heat** and add the lemon juice, Worcestershire sauce, 1 teaspoon salt and parsley.
- **Serve the almond-butter sauce over the halibut.**

Pecan Encrusted Halibut with Satsuma Sauce

Pecans and satsumas are wonderful autumn crops in Louisiana. The satsuma is a locally grown easy-peel orange that is both tart and sweet. This preparation of halibut is designed to be served with "Satsuma Sauce" (Page 169). Tangerines are a good substitute for satsumas. Serve the sauce on the side to keep the fish crispy on the plate. The pecan crust browns quickly and when it has browned the halibut will be finished cooking. This dish takes a bit of extra effort but the results are well worth it.

Serve with mashed potatoes and a steamed green vegetable (green peas, broccoli or snow peas). This dish is suitable for a special meal such as a birthday or anniversary.

Ingredients--

1-1/2 cups pecans
1 cup satsuma segments, membranes and seeds removed, cut into 3/4-inch pieces
1/2 cup flour
1 Tablespoon salt
1 Tablespoon cayenne pepper
2 eggs, beaten
4 six-ounce pieces of halibut (skin and dark areas removed)
1/2 cup unsalted butter
3/4 cup vegetable oil

Pecan Encrusted Halibut with Satsuma Sauce

Procedure --

- **Toast the pecans** in a microwave oven for 4 minutes and allow to cool.
- **Process 1 cup of pecans** in a blender or food processor to produce "pecan flour" and reserve. Process only until the nuts become a "flour". Longer processing will produce pecan butter. A few larger pieces will remain.
- **Crush the remaining pecans** to about 1/4-inch pieces and reserve.
- **Prepare the satsumas** and reserve.
- **Mix the flour, salt** and cayenne pepper thoroughly.
- **Put the pecan flour, flour mixture** and beaten eggs, each into separate bowls.
- **Remove excess moisture from the halibut portions** with a paper towel.
- **Heat the butter and oil together** in a frying pan to 325° F.
- **Coat the halibut portions** in the flour mixture, dip in the beaten egg, coat with pecan flour and place in the hot oil.
- **Fry the halibut on one side** until the pecan crust becomes dark brown. This happens more quickly than it does when using only flour. Turn the halibut and cook until the crust is finished.
- **Garnish the halibut** with the reserved satsuma pieces and reserved pecan pieces.

Grilled Salmon and Halibut

While grilled fish can be served with different marinades and sauces, the fundamentals of grilling remain the same. Following are four methods for grilling fish.

Salmon and halibut have quite different textures and oil contents which present different needs when grilling. Salmon is reasonably forgiving when grilled. Its relatively high fat content helps keep it moist and also helps it brown a bit. Slightly browned, salmon will be well done. Halibut requires greater attention. Although halibut will take on grill marks, it generally will not brown, even if coated in oil. By the time it does brown, it will be very overcooked. Hence, cook halibut only to an internal temperature of 145^0 F.

Basic Grilled Fish 1 -- Skin removed, cooked directly on grill

This method can be used with fish that is not marinated or fish that is marinated in a marinade containing oil that will help prevent the fish from sticking to the grill. If the fish is marinated, omit oiling the fish prior to grilling but do oil the grill surface. Serve with one of the sauces in the sauce section if not using a marinade.

Ingredients--

2-inch sections of salmon fillet (skin and pin bones removed) or sections of halibut (skin and dark areas removed), serving sized and trimmed to about 1-inch thick
1/3 cup extra virgin olive oil
1/2 teaspoon salt
1/2 teaspoon cracked black pepper

Procedure--

- **Prepare the grill** to have a medium heat with white coals.
- **Oil the grill surface** with olive oil.
- **Oil the surface of fish,** season with salt and pepper (or remove from marinade) and place skin side down on the grill.
- **Cook for 2 minutes,** turn 45 degrees and cook for an additional 2 minutes. This will give grill marks on the side that will be served facing up.
- **Oil the bone side surface of fish** and turn the fish over.
- **Grill until the fish is opaque throughout,** about 4 to 6 minutes.

Basic Grilled Salmon 2 -- Skin on, cooked directly on grill

Similar to "Basic Grilled Fish--1", this method can be used with fish that is not marinated or fish that is marinated in a marinade containing oil that will help prevent the fish from sticking to the grill. If the fish is marinated, omit oiling the fish prior to grilling but do oil the grill surface. The basic difference is that the salmon skin can be cooked until crispy and served facing up for a nice presentation. Alternately, the fish can be removed from the skin as it is removed from the grill. Since halibut skin is not suitable for grilling, this recipe is only for salmon.

Ingredients--

2-inch sections of salmon fillet (skin left on but scales and pin bones removed)
1/4 cup extra virgin olive oil
1/4 teaspoon salt
1/4 cup cracked black pepper

Procedure--

- **Marinade the fish** according to marinade instructions.
- **Prepare the grill** to have a medium heat with white coals.
- **Oil the grill surface** with olive oil.

To serve with crispy skin

- **Oil the surface of the fish,** season with salt and pepper (or remove from marinade) and place skin side down on grill.
- **Cook for 3 minutes,** turn the fish 45 degrees and cook for an additional 3 minutes. This will give grill marks on the side that will be served facing up.
- **Turn the skin side up** and cook until the fish is opaque throughout and flakes with a fork, 4 to 6 minutes.

Or, to serve without the skin, after the third step

- **Place the bone side down first,** cook for 2 minutes, turn 45 degrees and cook for 2 more minutes to produce grill marks.
- **Turn the skin side down** and cook for 6 to 8 minutes.
- **Remove the fish with a wide spatula** by separating the meat from the skin, leaving the skin on the grill for later cleaning.

Basic Grilled Fish 3 -- Skin removed, cooked in shallow container

This method is useful in preventing the fish from sticking to the grill especially so when a marinade lacks oil. Also, the container helps keep a marinade on the fish.

Ingredients--

2-inch sections of salmon fillet (skin and pin bones removed) or sections of halibut (skin and dark areas removed), serving sized and trimmed to about 1 inch thick
1/3 cup extra virgin olive oil
1/4 teaspoon salt
1/4 teaspoon cracked black pepper

Procedure--

- **Marinate the fish** according to marinade instructions.
- **Prepare the grill** to have a medium heat with white coals.
- **Mold a double layer of aluminum foil** into a shallow "bowl" that will hold the fish and some marinade. Form the bowl with the shiny side inside the fold. (The shiny side will reflect heat away from the fish).
- **Place the fish into the foil bowl on the grill,** brush the fish with oil and season with salt and pepper, or spoon some marinade onto the fish.
- **Cook with the grill cover down,** without turning, until the fish is opaque throughout and flakes, 10 to 12 minutes or until the internal temperature is 145° F.

Basic Grilled Fish 4 -- Skin removed, cooked on a plank

This method can be used with fish that is marinated without oil, although oil can be used. During cooking, the planks will produce smoke that will lightly flavor the fish. Grilling planks are available in many grocery stores. Most are either cedar or maple. Planks can be made of the same woods used for smoking fish. They should be planed to be about 1/2 inch thick. If they are 8 x 18 inches wide, they will hold eight portions.

Ingredients--

Grilling planks
2-inch sections of salmon fillet (skin and pin bones removed) or sections of halibut (skin and dark areas removed), serving sized and trimmed to about 1 inch thick
marinade, or
1/3 cup extra virgin olive oil
1/4 teaspoon salt
1/4 teaspoon cracked black pepper

Basic Grilled Fish 4

Procedure--

- **Soak the planks in water** for at least 1 hour.
- **Marinate the fish** according to marinade instructions.
- **Prepare the grill** to have a medium heat with white coals.
- **Drain the planks** and place the fish onto them. Place the planks onto the grill and spoon marinade over the fish or brush the fish with olive oil and season with salt and pepper.
- **Cook with the grill cover down,** without turning, until the fish is opaque throughout and flakes, 10 to 12 minutes or until the internal temperature is 145° F.

Grilling Marinades

While these marinades are designed for grilling, they are also suitable for pan-broiled preparations. Using marinades greatly expands the range of flavors that can be explored with grilled fish. Consider the flavors of the marinade when selecting the side dishes that will be served with the fish.

Asian Basil Marinade

Basil with a background of Asian flavors brings a fresh summer taste to either salmon or halibut.

Ingredients--

1/2 cup rice vinegar
1/2 cup extra virgin olive oil
8 green onions, both white and green portions cut to 1/8-inch rounds
2 Tablespoons sesame oil
2 Tablespoons soy sauce
2 Tablespoons dark brown sugar
5 Tablespoons fresh basil, chopped
1 teaspoon chill-garlic paste
1 teaspoon salt
1 teaspoon cracked black pepper

Procedure--

- **Mix all the ingredients** in a non-reactive bowl (glass or stainless steel).
- **Cover the fish with marinade.**
- **Marinade the fish** for about 30 minutes but no longer than 45 minutes as the mixture will soften the fish.
- **Grill the fish** according to one of the grilling methods. After the fish has been turned (methods 1 or 2 and at the beginning for methods 3 or 4) spoon ample marinade onto the fish.
- **Add marinade again** once or twice while cooking.

Pear Ginger Marinade

This is a wonderfully fruity marinade that brings out the flavor of the fish. Be sure to use ripe juicy pears since they are the star of this marinade.

Ingredients--

1/2 cup white balsamic vinegar
1/2 cup extra virgin olive oil
1/2 ripe pear, chopped to 1/8 to 1/4-inch cubes
3 Tablespoons fresh ginger, grated
1 teaspoon salt
1 teaspoon cracked black pepper

Procedure--

- **Mix the all ingredients** in a non-reactive bowl (glass or stainless steel).
- **Cover the fish with marinade.**
- **Marinate the fish** for about 30 minutes but no longer than 45 minutes as the mixture will soften the fish.
- **Grill the fish** according to one of the grilling methods. After the fish has been turned (methods 1 or 2 and at the beginning for methods 3 or 4) spoon ample marinade onto the fish.
- **Add marinade again** once or twice while cooking.

Honey Tangerine Marinade

Fruit makes a great base for a marinade and tangerine is one of the best. Sweetened with a light honey such a Pacific Coast fireweed honey, and spiced with a bit of ginger, this marinade is ideal for enhancing the flavor of salmon or halibut.

Ingredients--

1/2 cup honey
1/2 cup extra virgin olive oil
1 tangerine, peeled, segment removed from membranes, seeded and cut to 1/4-inch cubes with a very sharp knife
2 Tablespoons fresh ginger, grated
2 Tablespoons soy sauce
1/2 teaspoon Tabasco sauce

Procedure--

- **Mix all the ingredients** in a non-reactive bowl (glass or stainless steel).
- **Cover the fish with marinade.**
- **Marinate the fish** for about 30 minutes but no longer than 45 minutes as the mixture will soften the fish.
- **Grill the fish** according to one of the grilling methods. After the fish has been turned (methods 1 or 2 and at the beginning for methods 3 or 4) spoon ample marinade onto the fish.
- **Add marinade again** once or twice while cooking.

Lemon Rosemary Marinade

Lemon is, of course, perfect for fish. The rosemary brings a bright herbal tone to the marinade.

Ingredients--

3/4 cup extra virgin olive oil
2 cloves garlic, minced
1 Tablespoon fresh rosemary, finely chopped
juice of 1 lemon
1 Tablespoon honey
1 teaspoon salt

Procedure--

- **Mix the all ingredients** in a non-reactive bowl (glass or stainless steel).
- **Cover the fish with marinade.**
- **Marinade the fish** for about 30 minutes but no longer than 45 minutes as the mixture will soften the fish.
- **Grill the fish** according to one of the grilling methods. After the fish has been turned (methods 1 or 2 and at the beginning for methods 3 or 4) spoon ample marinade onto the fish.
- **Add marinade again** once or twice while cooking.

Fish Burgers

Fish served as a burger is a clear winner. Fish burgers can be served in a bun, on greens as a light meal or with side dishes such as "Potato Salad with Sour Cream, Chives and Smoked Salmon" (Page 51) without the smoked salmon. Since the flavor of salmon is more robust, it is better suited to the stronger flavor profiles of some of the following recipes. However, both salmon and halibut can be used for all of these recipes. All the recipes in this section will make four large burgers.

Since fish lacks the fat content of meat, fish burgers will not be as moist as beef hamburgers. However, their flavor is marvelous and a bit of sauce more than makes up for the comparative dryness.

Basic Salmon Burgers

This burger is intended to be served on hamburger buns with lettuce, sliced tomatoes and onions, catsup or mustard. A slice of cheese can be melted on the burger under a broiler, or if the burger has been cooked in a frying pan, place two Tablespoons of water into the pan, cover the pan and melt the cheese with the steam for about 2 minutes as the cooking is finishing.

Ingredients--

1-1/2 pounds salmon fillet (skin and pin bones removed)
1 egg
1 teaspoon salt
1 teaspoon cracked black pepper
1/2 cup panko bread crumbs, unseasoned
5 green onions, both white and green parts,
cut into 1/8-inch rounds
1/4 cup flour
1/2 cup extra virgin olive oil

Procedure--

- **Combine 3/4 pound of the salmon,** cut into chunks, the egg, salt and pepper in a food processer* and process until smooth.
- **Add 3/4 of pound the salmon,** cut into chunks and pulse, leaving the added salmon in small pieces of about 1/4 inch.
- **Remove the mixture from the processor** to a bowl and fold in the bread crumbs and green onions.
- **Form into 4 patties,** press lightly into the flour.
- **Grill, broil or sauté in olive oil,** 4 to 5 minutes on one side, then turn for an additional 4 to 5 minutes until both sides are golden brown.

*Although I call for using a food processor, I usually mince the fish with a knife to save washing the processor.

Asian Salmon Burgers

This burger compliments the flavor of the salmon. Serve on hamburger buns with "Kaffir Lime Sauce" (Page 173) or "Creamy Lime Sauce" (Page 174) with lettuce and tomato, or serve on a bed of lettuce with either sauce.

Ingredients--

1-1/2 pounds salmon fillet (skin and pin bones removed)
1 egg
1 teaspoon sesame oil
2 teaspoons soy sauce
1 teaspoon fish sauce
1 teaspoon lemon grass, white part only, finely chopped
1 teaspoon chili-garlic paste
2 Tablespoons fresh ginger
1/2 cup panko bread crumbs, unseasoned
5 green onions, both white and green parts,
cut into 1/8-inch rounds

Procedure--

- **Combine 3/4 pound of the salmon,** cut into chunks, the egg, sesame oil, soy sauce, fish sauce, lemon grass, chili-garlic paste and ginger in a food processer and process until smooth.
- **Add 3/4 pound of the salmon,** cut into chunks and pulse, leaving the added salmon in small pieces, about 1/4 inch.
- **Remove the mixture from the processor** to a bowl and fold in bread crumbs and green onions.
- **Form into 4 patties.**
- **Grill, broil or sauté** in olive oil, 4 to 5 minutes on one side, then turn and cook for an additional 4 to 5 minutes.

Basic Halibut Burgers

Simple seasonings allow the subtle flavor of halibut to shine. Serve on hamburger buns with "Remoulade Sauce" (Page 175), with lettuce and tomato or serve on a bed of lettuce with "Remoulade Sauce".

Ingredients--

1 1/2 pounds of halibut fillets (skin and dark areas removed), cut into 1-1/2 inch pieces
1 egg, beaten
1 teaspoon salt
1 /4 teaspoon cayenne pepper
1/2 cup panko bread crumbs
1 cup green onion, both white and green parts

Procedure--

- **Combine 3/4 pound of the halibut** pieces, the egg, salt and cayenne pepper in a food processor and process until smooth.
- **Add 3/4 pound of the halibut** and pulse, leaving the added halibut in about 1/4 inch pieces.
- **Remove the mixture from the processor** to a bowl and fold in the bread crumbs and green onions.
- **Form into 4 patties.**
- **Grill, broil or sauté** in olive oil, 4 to 5 minutes on one side, then turn and cook for an additional 4 to 5 minutes until patties are browned and cooked through.

Thai Style Salmon Burgers

Fish burgers can be easily enhanced with herbs and spices. This burger features the wonderful tastes of Thailand.

These burgers go well on a salad made with lettuce, sliced mango and sliced avocado. A simple dressing for the salad can be made with 1/2 cup mayonnaise, 1/2 cup Greek yogurt, 1 teaspoon salt, a dash of Tabasco sauce and the juice of 1 lime. The burgers also can be served on a bun with some of the dressing alongside the salad as an accompaniment.

Ingredients--

1-1/2 pounds salmon fillet (skin and pin bones removed)
1 egg, beaten
1/2 teaspoon fish sauce
3 Tablespoons shallot, coarsely chopped
2 Tablespoons lemon grass, white portion chopped very fine
1-1/2 teaspoons chili-garlic paste
2 Tablespoons fresh galangal (Asian ginger) or ginger
3/4 cup panko bread crumbs, unseasoned

Procedure--

- **Combine 3/4 pound of the salmon,** cut into chunks, the egg, fish sauce, shallot, lemon grass, chili-garlic paste and ginger in a food processor and process until smooth.
- **Add 3/4 pound of the salmon,** cut into chunks and pulse, leaving the added salmon in small pieces, about 1/4 inch.
- **Remove the mixture from the processor** to a bowl and fold in the bread crumbs.
- **Form into 4 patties.**
- **Grill, broil or sauté** in olive oil, 4 to 5 minutes on one side, then turn and cook for an additional 4 to 5 minutes until the patties are browned and cooked through.

Thai Style Salmon Burgers with Kaffir Lime Leaves

The use of kaffir lime leaves (see Page 24 for sources) is unique to Thai cooking. Their bright aromatic flavor enhances the flavor of the salmon.

Dressing the burger, either on a bun or a salad, with a sauce made with 1/2 cup Greek yogurt, 1/2 cup sour cream, 2 kaffir lime leaves, mid-rib removed and very finely chopped, and salt to taste heightens the fresh taste.

Ingredients--

1-1/2 pounds salmon fillet (skin and pin bones removed)
1 egg, beaten
1/2 teaspoon fish sauce
3 kaffir lime leaves, mid-rib removed
1 Tablespoon fresh garlic, minced
1 teaspoon chili-garlic paste
1 teaspoon cracked black pepper
3/4 cup panko bread crumbs, unseasoned

Procedure--

- **Combine 3/4 pound of the salmon,** cut into chunks, the egg, fish sauce, kaffir lime leaves, garlic, chili-garlic paste and black pepper in a food processor and process until smooth.
- **Add 3/4 pound of the salmon,** cut into chunks and pulse, leaving the added salmon in small pieces of about 1/4 inch.
- **Remove the mixture from the processor** to a bowl and fold in the bread crumbs.
- **Form into 4 patties.**
- **Grill, broil or sauté** in olive oil, 4 to 5 minutes on one side, then turn and cook for an additional 4 to 5 minutes.

A Few Selected Side Dishes

Most of the sides I have suggested are familiar preparations, such as steamed vegetables or mashed potatoes. The few sides in this section are either a bit unusual or are special favorites of mine that deserve to be presented as recommended recipes.

Sushi Rice

Sushi rice requires a somewhat different preparation than typical white rice. The final product should be sticky so that it can be formed into balls for sushi or easily eaten with chop sticks.

Serve in "Halibut Sashimi Bowl" (Page 26), or sprinkle with black or toasted sesame seeds and serve under "Asian Poached Salmon" (Page 83).

Ingredients--

1 cup sushi rice
1-1/4 cups water
2 Tablespoons sweet rice wine vinegar

Procedure--

- **Rinse the rice in cold water.** Repeat until the rinse water is clear.
- **Bring the water to a boil** and add the rice.
- **Reduce heat to very low,** cover and cook 20 minutes.
- **Remove from heat** and let sit covered for 10 minutes.
- **Mix well with vinegar.**

Orange Pecan Salad

This salad, served with "Orange Honey Salad Dressing" (Page 156), is a winner with both adults and children. The sweet honey, the slight acid of the orange and the rich taste of the toasted nuts make a special combination.

Ingredients--

4 cups mixed greens (some combination of "sweet" and "bitter" greens such as romaine lettuce, spinach and arugula)
sections cut from 2 oranges (navel oranges, satsumas or tangerines)
1/2 cup pecans, toasted

Procedure--

- **Toast the pecans** in a microwave for 3-1/2 minutes.
- **Mix the greens,** orange sections and pecans.
- **Dress with** "Orange Honey Salad Dressing" (Page 156).

Rice with Green Peas and Toasted Pecans

Many of the fish preparations in this book benefit from being served with a carbohydrate and a vegetable. This dish fills both needs. It is particularly good with many of the broiled fish recipes. It is fast and easy for a quick meal and can be served either hot or at room temperature. The dish is intended to be a bit peppery.

Many of these recipes call for serving on cooked white rice. The method for cooking rice in this recipe works perfectly every time.

Ingredients--

1 cup white rice
2 cups water
2 cups pecans
2 cups green peas, fresh or frozen
1/2 cup extra virgin olive oil
1 teaspoon salt
1 Tablespoons cracked black pepper

Procedure--

- **Boil the water, add the rice** and return to a boil and reduce heat to very low and cover.
- **Cook for 20 minutes** without removing cover.
- **Remove from heat** and fluff with fork.
- **Spread the pecans on a plate** and microwave on high for 4 minutes to toast them.
- **Steam the peas until tender.**
- **Blanch the peas in ice water** so that they remain bright green and drain.
- **Combine the cooked rice,** peas, pecans, olive oil, salt and pepper.

Refried Potatoes

This is an upscale way to prepare fried potatoes. Use medium heat to prevent the butter from burning and continue cooking until the potatoes are lightly browned.

These potatoes can be served with many dishes and work especially well with "Pan Fried Halibut with Two Sauces" (Page 112).

Ingredients--

4 cups red potatoes, peeled and cut into 1/2-inch cubes
4 Tablespoons unsalted butter
salt to taste
1/4 cup Worcestershire sauce
1/2 cup parsley, chopped

Procedure--

- **Boil the potatoes** until tender but firm and drain.
- **Sauté the potatoes** in the butter on medium heat, turning often until browned.
- **Season with salt to taste.**
- **Fold in the Worcestershire sauce** and parsley.

Cheesy Creamy Grits

These grits are designed to be served with "New Orleans Style Barbecued Salmon Strips" (Page 93) and "Barbecue Sauce" (Page 161). If used for another purpose, replace the fish stock with chicken stock. The recipe uses white cheddar cheese. I prefer "Cougar Gold" from the creamery at Washington State University. It is excellent and ships well since it is made in a sealed can. It may be purchased from their website, but is not available for shipping in the summer months.

Ingredients--

1-1/2 cups fish stock
1 cup India pale ale with Cascade hops
1 teaspoon salt
3/4 cup white grits
1/4 cup heavy cream
3 Tablespoons unsalted butter
1 teaspoon cracked black pepper
1-1/2 cups white cheddar cheese, grated

Procedure--

- **Bring the fish stock,** ale and salt to boil in a sauce pan.
- **Slowly stir in the grits** and cook to a thick consistency according to package instructions.
- **Remove from heat** and stir in the cream, butter, pepper and cheddar cheese.

Sauces and Dressings

Very often, it is the sauce that makes the dish. Sauces add complexity of flavor and subtlety of texture, and most of them are easy to make. Many of the fish preparations in this cookbook are designed to be served with specific sauces which are referenced in the general comments about the recipes. However, many of the sauces could be used with many other recipes sourced in this book and elsewhere. For example, the "Remoulade Sauce" (Page 175) could be used to dress a salad or as an accompaniment to boiled shrimp or boiled crab.

Lime Ginger Sashimi Sauce

The simplicity of small pieces of raw fish ("Halibut Sashimi Bowl with Lime Ginger Sauce", Page 26) on sushi rice requires a flavorful sauce. Serve this sauce to the side so that a lot or a little can be used as desired.

Ingredients--

2 teaspoons soy sauce
1 teaspoon sesame oil
1 teaspoon lime juice
zest from 1/2 lime
1 Tablespoon dark brown sugar

Procedure--

- **Whisk all ingredients together.**

Mustard Dill Sauce (*Hovmästarsås*)

> *This Swedish classic is the traditional sauce served with an appetizer of "Gravlox" (Page 37) and boiled potatoes.*

Ingredients--

2 Tablespoons sugar
6 Tablespoons fresh dill, chopped
1/2 cup Dijon mustard
1 Tablespoon honey
1 Tablespoon red wine vinegar
1/2 cup extra virgin olive oil
salt and cracked black pepper to taste

Procedure--

- **Mix the sugar and dill.**
- **Add the mustard,** honey and vinegar.
- **Whisk together** and slowly add the oil while continuing to whisk.
- **Season with salt and pepper to taste.**

Parmesan Cream Sauce with Smoked Salmon

This sauce is used to finish pasta and is intended to be used with "Smoked Salmon with Fettuccine in Parmesan Cream Sauce" (Page 44). Of course, if the salmon is omitted, it can be used to sauce any pasta.

Ingredients--

1/4 pound unsalted butter
6 to 8 cups of cooked pasta
2 cups thick cream
1 cup freshly grated parmesan cheese
zest and juice of 1 lemon
1 teaspoon nutmeg
1 teaspoon cracked black pepper
dash Tabasco sauce
3 cups "Hot Smoked" salmon, flaked
1/4 cup parsley, chopped

Procedure--

- **Melt the butter** in a large frying pan.
- **On medium heat,** add cooked pasta and stir to coat.
- **Add the cream** and bring to a boil.
- **Add the cheese,** lemon zest and juice, nutmeg, pepper and Tabasco sauce.
- **Fold gently until the cheese is melted** and the sauce is thick.
- **Remove from heat** and fold in the salmon.
- **Place on serving plates** and sprinkle with the parsley.

Orange Honey Salad Dressing

This salad dressing is designed for "Orange Pecan Salad" (Page 146) but it can be used on any salad containing fruit. Since it is sweet, it is a favorite of both adults and children. It is my standard house dressing when I include fruit in a salad.

Ingredients--

1/2 cup orange juice
1/4 cup honey
2 Tablespoons extra virgin olive oil
1/2 Tablespoon cracked black pepper
1/2 teaspoon salt
4 to 6 dashes of Tabasco sauce according to taste

Procedure--

- **Shake all ingredients** in a closed jar or whisk until blended.
- **Dress the salad** and serve.

Meunière Sauce

This is a classic French sauce that has a rich hardy flavor. Serve with "Smoked Salmon Cheesecake" (Page 47) or "Pan-Fried Halibut with Two Sauces" (Page 112).

Ingredients--

1 cup "Basic Fish Stock" (Page10)
1 tablespoon fresh garlic, minced
3/4 pound unsalted butter
2 tablespoons flour
1/4 cup Worcestershire sauce
1/4 teaspoon salt

Procedure--

- **Combine the stock and garlic,** boil and reduce to a simmer.
- **In a separate pan,** melt 3 tablespoons of butter, add the flour and whisk until the mixture foams, forming a very light roux.
- **Whisk the roux into the stock** until smooth.
- **Cut the remaining butter** into chunks and add them to the sauce, whisking continually.
- **When the butter is melted,** remove from heat and whisk in the Worcestershire sauce and salt.

Cobb Salad Dressing

This is a refreshing salad dressing that can be used on many savory salads. It works well on "Cobb Salad with Smoked Salmon" (Page 49).

Ingredients--

1/4 cup water
1/4 cup red wine vinegar
1 teaspoon sugar
1 teaspoon lemon juice
2 teaspoons salt
3/4 teaspoon cracked black pepper
3/4 teaspoon Worcestershire sauce
1/2 teaspoon dry ground yellow mustard
1 clove of garlic, minced
1/4 cup extra virgin olive oil
3/4 cup canola oil

Procedure--

- **Combine all ingredients** except oils and mix well.
- **Slowly whisk in oils.**
- **Mix well again just before dressing the salad.**

Cucumber Tarragon Sauce

This bright flavorful sauce brings the taste of summer to the table. Serve on "Salmon Loaf with Cucumber Tarragon Sauce" (Page 87) or on "Basic Salmon Burgers" (Page 135).

Ingredients--

1/2 cup mayonnaise
1/2 cup sour cream
3/4 cup cucumber, peeled, seeded and diced to 1/4 inch
2 Tablespoons fresh tarragon, minced
salt and cracked pepper to taste

Procedure--

- **Mix all ingredients** and chill before serving.

Lemon Butter Sauce

This light, bright sauce is richly lemon but because of the honey lacks the bitterness that lemon can bring to a dish. Serve with "Pan Broiled Salmon Encrusted with Sliced Almonds" (Page 74).

Ingredients--

1/4 cup white wine
zest and juice of 1 large lemon
1/4 cup heavy cream
3/4 cup unsalted butter
honey, salt and white pepper to taste

Procedure--

- **Mix the wine and lemon** juice in a small pan, heat and reduce by 1/3.
- **Mix in the cream** and simmer 3 minutes.
- **Cut the butter into sections** and whisk into the mixture until melted.
- **Add the lemon zest,** and adjust the bitterness of the lemon with a small amount (1/4 to 1 Tablespoon) of honey to taste.
- **Season with salt and pepper to taste.**

Barbecue Sauce

This is a classical southern barbecue sauce adjusted to serve with fish and given a Pacific Northwestern flair with the addition of the ale with Cascade hops. Serve with "New Orleans Style Barbecued Salmon Strips" (Page 93) and "Creamy Cheesy Grits" (Page 151).

Ingredients--

8 Tablespoons unsalted butter
4 cloves garlic, minced
1 teaspoon cayenne pepper
1/2 teaspoon salt
1 teaspoon cracked black pepper
1 teaspoon dried or 1 Tablespoon fresh thyme, chopped
1 teaspoon dried or 1 Tablespoon fresh oregano, chopped
1 teaspoon red pepper flakes
1 cup "Basic Fish Stock" (Page 10)
1/2 cup West Coast style India pale ale with Cascade hops
1/4 cup Worcestershire sauce

Procedure--

- **Melt the butter** in a small sauce pan on medium heat.
- **Add the garlic and sauté** on medium heat for 1 minute. Do not brown either butter or garlic.
- **Stirring constantly,** add the cayenne pepper, salt, black pepper, thyme, oregano and pepper flakes.

Sauté 20

seconds.

- **Add the stock and ale,** increase the heat to high and bring the mixture to a boil.
- **Reduce the mixture** to about 1/2 the volume and add the Worcestershire sauce.
- **Reduce the mixture** to about 1/3 the original volume, and serve.

Tarragon Hollandaise Sauce

This is a basic hollandaise sauce enriched with the flavor of tarragon. It is designed to serve with "Halibut Cheeks stuffed with Tarragon Salmon Mousse" (Page 106) but could also be served with salmon or halibut poached in a broth with tarragon or broiled.

A stainless steel or Pyrex bowl placed over a pan with boiling water makes an acceptable double boiler.

Ingredients--

2 egg yolks
1/2 pound unsalted butter, cut into 1/2-inch slices
juice of 1/2 lemon
1/2 teaspoon salt
4 dashes of Tabasco sauce
3 Tablespoons fresh tarragon leaves, minced

Procedure--

- **Bring water to a boil** in the bottom of a double boiler.
- **Place egg yolks** into top of a double boiler.
- **As the yolks begin to heat** constantly whisk, adding the butter 3 or 4 pieces at a time until all the butter is incorporated.
- **Remove from heat.**
- **Continue whisking** and add the lemon juice, salt, Tabasco sauce and tarragon.

White Sauce for Fish Tacos

This sauce is rich in the flavors of Mexico; lime, jalapeño pepper, oregano and cumin. It is designed to be served on fish tacos made with "Fish Tacos with Beer Battered Deep Fried Halibut" (Page 108).

Ingredients--

1/2 cup plain yogurt
1/2 cup mayonnaise
zest and juice of 1 lime
1 jalapeño pepper, seeded and minced
1 teaspoon capers, minced
1-1/2 teaspoons fresh oregano leaves, minced
1/2 teaspoon ground cumin
1-1/2 teaspoons fresh dill, stems removed and leaves minced
1 teaspoon ground cayenne pepper
1 teaspoon salt

Procedure--

- **Mix all ingredients** and refrigerate until use.

Tartar Sauce

While this tartar sauce can be made with store bought mayonnaise it is better with homemade "Basic Mayonnaise" (Page 172). Serve with "Pan Fried Halibut with Two Sauces" (Page 114) instead of the two sauces, "Yakutat Halibut Nuggets" (Page 115) or on any of the burgers in the burger section (Pages 134 to 144).

Ingredients--

1-1/2 cups mayonnaise
4-5 sweet gherkins or
3 Tablespoons sweet pickle relish
4 green onions, thinly sliced using both white and green portions
1 Tablespoon capers, drained and chopped
1 Tablespoon fresh parsley, finely chopped
3 Tablespoons fresh tarragon, finely chopped,
or 1 Tablespoon dried tarragon
1 Tablespoon Dijon mustard
1/4 teaspoon cider vinegar
salt and cracked black pepper to taste

Procedure--

- **Mix all ingredients.**
- **Season with salt and pepper to taste.**
- **Refrigerate until use.**

Pecan Butter Sauce

This sauce is designed to place on cooked fish just before serving. The hot fish will melt the butter which will spread the sauce. Serve with "Pan Fried Halibut with Two Sauces" (Page 112).

Ingredients--

1/2 cup pecans
4 Tablespoons unsalted butter, softened
2 Tablespoons red onion, finely chopped
1/2 teaspoon Tabasco sauce
1/2 teaspoon garlic, minced

Procedure--

- **Toast the pecans** in a microwave for 4 minutes.
- **Cool and finely chop pecans** to 1/8 inch pieces.
- **Mix the pecans,** butter, onion, Tabasco sauce and garlic.

Fish Velouté Sauce with White Wine and Tarragon

A velouté sauce is a basic French sauce made of fish stock thickened with a roux. It needs additional ingredients to produce a finished sauce. This sauce begins with a basic sauce using "Halibut Skin Fish Stock" (Page 12), and is finished with white wine and tarragon. It is designed to be served with "Pan Roasted Halibut" (Page 114), although it is suitable for several other halibut preparations as well. If you pair this sauce with a salmon preparation use "Salmon Skin Fish Stock" (Page 14).

Ingredients--

3 Tablespoons unsalted butter
3 Tablespoons flour
1 cup "Halibut Skin Fish Stock" (Page 12)
1/2 cup white wine
salt to taste
3 Tablespoons fresh tarragon, minced

Procedure--

- **On high heat** whisk the butter and flour until the mixture foams, forming a very light roux.
- **Whisk in the fish stock and wine** and simmer until thickened.
- **Remove from heat,** add the tarragon and salt to taste.

Honey Mustard Sauce

This classic sauce is both easy to make and delicious. Serve with "Yakutat Halibut Nuggets" (Page 115) as an appetizer, as a kid's meal while the adults have something else or on salad greens as a light main course.

Ingredients--

2 Tablespoons honey
2 Tablespoons Dijon Mustard
1 Tablespoon mayonnaise
1/4 teaspoon Tabasco sauce

Procedure--

- **Whisk all ingredients together.**

Satsuma Sauce

This sauce is designed to be served with "Pecan Encrusted Halibut with Satsuma Sauce" (Page 118). Satsumas are a Louisiana grown easy-peel orange that is both tart and sweet. They do not ship well so are not nationally available. However, tangerines are similar and can be used as a substitute for satsumas in this preparation. Serve the sauce in a separate small bowl for each guest, rather than on the fish, so that the coating will stay crisp.

Ingredients--

2 cups satsuma juice
1/2 cup unsalted butter
2 Tablespoons honey
1 teaspoon salt
1 teaspoon cracked black pepper
1 Tablespoon corn starch

Procedure --

- **Heat the satsuma juice,** butter, honey, salt and pepper to a simmer.
- **Simmer and reduce** the volume to 1/2.
- **Remove about 3/4 cup of the mixture** to a small bowl and whisk in the corn starch.
- **Return the corn starch mixture** to the satsuma juice mixture and whisk while heating until the sauce has thickened.

Fig Chutney

Figs are a wonderful summer crop but most varieties do not last long after picking. Fortunately, they can be used to make chutney which is a perfect accompaniment to "Pan Broiled Halibut" (Page 99).

The chutney can be prepared and refrigerated for up to three weeks in advance or frozen for a year and used with pork and chicken as well as halibut.

Ingredients--

2 cups red wine vinegar
1/2 pound dark brown sugar
1 medium white onion, 1/4 inch dice
1/4 cup fresh ginger, grated
zest and juice from 1/2 lemon
1 cinnamon stick
3/4 teaspoon salt
1/2 teaspoon ground allspice
1/8 teaspoon ground cloves
1-1/4 pounds firm, slightly under ripe fresh figs,
rinsed, stems removed and halved

Procedure--

- **In a large saucepan combine the vinegar,** sugar, onion, ginger, lemon zest and juice, cinnamon stick, salt, allspice, and cloves and bring to a boil.
- **Reduce the heat to a simmer** and cook until the mixture is thickened and reduced by 2/3, forming a thick syrup. If the mixture becomes too thick, add 1/2 cup of water.
- **Add the figs** and cook gently until the figs are very soft and beginning to fall apart and most of the liquid they've given off has evaporated, about 30 minutes.
- **Remove the cinnamon stick** and transfer the chutney to a non-reactive container and allow to come to room temperature before serving or freezing.

Basic Mayonnaise

This homemade mayonnaise can be used in any preparation calling for mayonnaise. Tarragon, basil, chives or anther herb can be added to produce a fresh herbal taste that matches the dish served.

Ingredients--

2 egg yolks
1/4 cup extra virgin olive oil
1-3/4 cups peanut or canola oil
juice of 1 lemon
1/4 teaspoon Tabasco Sauce
salt and cracked black pepper to taste
herbs as desired, finely chopped

Procedure--

- **In a food processer,** blend the egg yolks for 3-4 pulses.
- **With the processer running,** pour a thin stream of olive oil and then canola oil until mixture begins to thicken.
- **With the processer running,** add the lemon juice and Tabasco sauce.
- **Remove to a bowl,** season with salt and pepper to taste and fold in herbs as desired.
- **Refrigerate until use.**

Kaffir Lime Sauce

Kaffir lime leaves provide one of the essential tastes of Thailand. Kaffir lime leaves are so special that one of my dogs is named "Kaffir".

Some high-end grocery stores or Asian markets may carry kaffir lime leaves. Small trees can be found as plants on the internet for sale that can and grown outside in a pot during summer and brought inside for the winter.

Serve this sauce on "Asian Salmon Burgers" (Page 137) or on grilled, poached or broiled salmon.

Ingredients--

3/4 cup mayonnaise
1/2 cup sour cream
juice of 1/2 lime
3 large kaffir lime leaves, veins removed
1/2 teaspoon salt

Procedure--

- **Place all ingredients into a food processor** or blender and process until the kaffir leaves are finely chopped.

Creamy Lime Sauce

Lime brings a nice fresh flavor to this sauce. Persian limes are good and Key limes are even better. If you use Key limes, use the zest and juice of five limes. Serve on "Asian Salmon Burgers" (Page 137) or grilled, poached or broiled salmon or halibut.

Ingredients--

3/4 cup mayonnaise
1/2 cup sour cream
zest of 1 lime
juice of 1/2 lime
1/2 teaspoon salt

Procedure--

- **Whisk all ingredients together.**

Remoulade Sauce

This version of Remoulade sauce is spectacular. Remoulade sauce is often used in South Louisiana for seafood, especially for fried oysters, boiled shrimp or fried or boiled crawfish. It could be used with many of the recipes in this book, such as "Yakutat Halibut Nuggets" (Page 115) as an appetizer, on salad greens as a dressing or on sandwiches with "Basic Halibut Burgers "(Page 139), "Basic Pan Broiled Salmon" (Page 71) or "Pan Broiled Halibut" (Page 99) with lettuce and tomato. After preparing, refrigerate for a day before use to allow flavors to blend. This sauce will keep refrigerated for 2 weeks.

Ingredients--

1/2 cup red onion, chopped
3/4 cup peanut oil
1/4 cup tarragon vinegar
1/2 cup prepared brown spicy mustard
2 teaspoons paprika
1/2 teaspoon cayenne pepper
2 teaspoons salt
2 medium cloves garlic
1/2 cup green onions, green and white parts, sliced to 1/4 inch

Procedure--

- **Combine all ingredients** except the green onions in a food processor and process until smooth.
- **Before serving,** fold in green onions.
- **Refrigerate until use.**

Made in United States
Troutdale, OR
07/26/2024

21548296R00106